the VISIONARY LEADER

How to inspire success from the top down

SUSAN BAGYURA

LIFESUCCESS PUBLISHING, LLC
8900 E Pinnacle Peak Road, Suite D240
Scottsdale, AZ 85255
Telephone: 800.473.7134
Fax: 480.661.1014
E-mail: admin@lifesuccesspublishing.com

ISBN: 978-1-59930-094-8

Cover : Fiona Dempsey & LifeSuccess Publishing
Layout: Fiona Dempsey & LifeSuccess Publishing

COMPANIES, ORGANIZATIONS,
INSTITUTIONS, AND INDUSTRY PUBLICATIONS:
*Quantity discounts are available on bulk purchases of this book for reselling,
educational purposes, subscription incentives, gifts,
sponsorship, or fundraising. Special books or book excerpts can also
be created to fit specific needs such as private labeling with your logo
on the cover and a message from a VIP printed inside.*
FOR MORE INFORMATION PLEASE CONTACT OUR
SPECIAL SALES DEPARTMENT AT
LIFESUCCESS PUBLISHING.

Dedication

I dedicate this book to my husband, Stefan, a great source of love and support for which I will always be grateful. A true visionary leader!

Acknowledgments

WITH THE KNOWLEDGE that we are the sum of all that has happened to us, it is with deepest gratitude that I wish to thank every person who has come into my life and has played a role to a greater or lesser extent in helping me in my journey of discovery.

I would like to acknowledge and express my gratitude particularly to the following people for their support and contributions in the creation of this book: my husband, Stefan, for his ongoing support, wisdom and input; Robert Sams, a true friend, a technical genius, and one of the most giving people I know, who has helped me enormously with his truthful guidance and profound insights in human behavior; and Daniel Santiago as it was his inspiration and creative way of evoking the ideas that are the foundation for this book, but it was his continued help and support during the production that kept me going.

It was just 3 short years ago that I learned about Bob Proctor. I was fortunate enough to be on coaching calls that Bob was conducting and very quickly, my life started to change. However, it has been in the last 1-1/2 years that my life has been totally transformed as I made it my mission to forge a close business relationship with LifeSuccess by becoming a LifeSuccess Consultant, purchasing the Massachusetts license for LifeSuccess and using the LifeSuccess programs as the basis for my coaching and consulting practice.

This decision has brought significant rewards, including the opportunity to work closely with some brilliant people in the LifeSuccess companies, such as Paul Martinelli, Carol Gates, Gina Hayden, Cheryl Fisher and my CCP Master Coach partner, Margaret Merrill.

Testimonials

Susan Bagyura's book is on-point, insightful, inspiring and actionable what more could one seek from a comprehensive instruction book on leadership development.
Gerry Robert,
Bestselling author of *The Millionaire Mindset*

Great coaching on how to develop effective leadership skills! The Visionary Leader is a must read for all who manage other people. Inspiring others is the way forward to top performance.
Germaine Porche' and Jed Niederer,
co-authors *Coach Anyone About Anything*
and the *Coaching Soup for the Cartoon Soul series*

Success, happiness and fulfillment all hinge on our ability to lead. We must effectively lead ourselves and others while fostering creative, mental and spiritual growth. The question remains..."How do we grow our leadership skills so that we powerfully inspire our own life and the lives of others?" Susan Bagyura has the answers. The Visionary Leader is insightful, honest and solidly packed with the information you need to reach the heights you envision. In your hands is the answer you've been searching for.
Margaret Merrill,
Author *Live the Life You Love;*
Discover Your Purpose and Live It With Intention

The power behind Susan's work lies not only in the road map she provides, but also in helping us see how truly inspirational and motivational a strong leader can be.
Robert LICHAL,
Retired Former Austrian Federal Minister of Defense.
Former Second President of the National Council
of the Austrian Parliament
Former Representative of the National Council and Federal Council
of the Austrian Parliament

This new book is a must read for CEOs, VP Level Executives and aspiring mid-level Managers. It tells how to make the bridge between being a good leader and a great leader.
Paul and Shelley Fox,
Authors of *Diamonds Demystified*

This book is a clear, concise guide for leadership development. This is more than a book for business. I recommend it to anybody who wants to be of service to others as it is the right formula for creating inner motivation.
Mark Plant,
Vice President Europe, Wright Line LLC

The Visionary Leader is far more fundamental and important than a book about leadership. It is about getting what you want in all aspects of life, including your business.
Paul Martinelli,
President, LifeSuccess Consultants

If you are newly in a leadership position, The Visionary Leader will chop years off your learning cycle. And even if you are an old pro, Susan Bagyura's insights will elevate you to new levels of effectiveness.
Dalia Lavon,
author of *The Magnetic CEO*....

The power behind Susan's work lies not only in the road map she provides, but also in helping us see how truly inspirational and motivational a strong leader can be.

David Butler,
author of *A Hand Up, Not A Hand Out*

I am a better manager, a more powerful leader, and a more understanding person as a result of The Visionary Leader. This book is written for people who want to play a bigger game.

Matt Allen,
author of Leverage Your IRA

This book is such a clear, concise guide for leadership development. This is more than a book for business. I recommend it to anybody who wants to be of service to others as it is the right formula for creating inner motivation.

Stephen and Karen Byrne,
authors of *S.O.S….. Systems of Success*

The leadership development concepts in The Visionary Leader will help you to be more successful in your business. Your results and goals will be far exceeded from this point forward.

Chris Snook,
author of *Burnout* and *Wealth Matters*

This book is loaded with valuable concepts and practical applications that assist you in those areas of your business that you may not have been able to impact yet. It shows you how to push through obstacles that have stopped your organization from realizing its full potential.
Janis Vos,
author of *The Success Tool Box*

Every business needs to be more in tune and in touch with its people. This book offers a quick road map to help us get there.
Buki Mosaku,
author of *The Skills to Pay the Bills…. And Then Some*

The concepts in The Visionary Leader will work for everyone and every business. I highly recommend this book and Susan Bagyura!
Dr. Maurizio Pupi,
European Business Director, Alliance Medical

Foreword

VISIONARY LEADERS ARE capable of looking beyond the superficial situations and circumstances of life, and develop the skill of looking deep into the heart of everyone whom they come in contact with, especially themselves. They are able to lead with courage and inspire others to cultivate their talents and abilities, while helping every one become aware of their true potential. This is a unique ability that, when developed, can transform a person's life, business, culture, and industry. I recommend you study this book, and each time you pick it up to read; think of your vision, your purpose, and your goals, because with great leadership comes great responsibility.

Your ability to effectively communicate with your colleagues, associates, employees, and business partners is of great importance. As your level of awareness increases, and you begin to maximize your potential, you can quickly and effortlessly cause other people to feel at ease in your presence, trust in your word, and want to do business with you. The visionary leader is one who walks humbly yet confidently, and who strives to continually develop their talents and abilities to the degree that they are successful in whatever they do.

As you move from chapter to chapter, you will become aware that Susan Bagyura is presenting you with important truths that are universal and will work for everyone. She has accumulated them from her own personal development, years of experience in the corporate environment, being a certified business coach and practitioner of powerful psychometric profiling tools, along with being a student of and a business partner with LifeSuccess. The combination of her ability to teach others to achieve their greatest potential and enlighten business professionals worldwide contributes to her overall effectiveness and adds intrinsic value to any individual or organization wishing to take their business to the next level and beyond.

If you're an executive looking to develop and improve your personal and professional effectiveness and influence, the Visionary Leader: How to Inspire Success from the Top Down will both enlighten and inspire you. Susan eloquently explains how Visionary Leaders become aware of, develop, and use their higher faculties of their mind to lead with discernment, wisdom, and confidence. If you want to alter and improve your results both personally and professionally, take to heart the principles and strategies that Susan Bagyura presents in this book. The ideas and concepts included in this book will dramatically impact your life and how you do business, both now and forever!

Bob Proctor
Bestselling author of *You Were Born Rich*

Table of Contents

Introduction

Why this Book is Important to Your Success

"Success is the progressive realization of a worthy goal or ideal."
- Earl Nightingale

YOU'VE SPENT YEARS of training and experience to get to the leadership position you now occupy, but maybe there are things you want to accomplish that seem to escape you. Of course, you're successful in every way, but do you always get the results you want in your organization? Many people have the instincts to be a leader, but they lack the knowledge that can make the difference between a good leader and a great leader. If this sounds familiar, then I have good news. As an experienced leadership and management coach, I believe my expertise in this book may just be the answer you're looking for.

Perhaps there are areas of your business that you haven't been able to impact yet. We can address those concerns together, and I can provide valuable concepts and practical applications that will assist you in those areas. Working together, you and I will identify and push through any obstacles that may stand in your way of realizing the full organizational potential of your business and will increase your productivity, income, and level of satisfaction.

From my years of working in business and marketing, I've learned that the path to reaching your goals can be littered with obstacles. If the path involves change, then many people will resist it. Change is one of the top three fears we experience, both in our personal lives and our business endeavors. This book shares keys to opening the doors to change, and it assists you as a manager to set organizational goals from which your employees and fellow managers will be able to grow. Being open to change is a win-win for everyone in your organization, starting with you.

I am going to share just a little bit at a time as you read this book. The purpose is not to overwhelm you with a great deal of information. Instead, this book will help to expand your awareness and share some of the things I know we can do to help your business grow in a meaningful way. If you apply these concepts to your own life and business, you will be amazed at the abundance you will attain financially.

I think you would agree that learning new concepts and changing anything requires a certain degree of confidence. If you have too little confidence, you might think you can't learn anything new. If you have a lot of experience and education, you may think you don't have anything else to learn. In my experience in working with and coaching people, most people seem to fall into one of those two categories. Some people think that they have all the answers, and they don't want to learn anything else. My understanding of business and my commitment to continuing education have helped me to be more successful in helping others to do the same.

The most successful organizations are those that follow an inspiring leader who has far-reaching influence and impact, one who leads a successful and profitable organization with a productive culture and nurtures the best in all its members, from the executive board room to the support staff. As a leader, you are able to get most of the results you want. But what about the areas you haven't been able to reach yet? I am part of your solution to reach those areas that itch but you can't quite scratch. The solution for your future lies in your hands.

You may remember the book, Jonathan Livingston Seagull written by Richard Bach in 1970. It is a popular fable about a seagull that entered another plane of existence to better his life, and then returned to teach the other gulls what he had learned. At one point Jonathan, the seagull, says, "I want to fly where no seagull has flown before. I want to know what there is to know about life!" Like him, you can choose to soar and explore a new life filled with success.

Chapter One

LEADERSHIP

Chapter One

LEADERSHIP

"The greatest discovery of my generation is that human beings can alter their lives by altering their attitudes of mind."
-- **William James**

THROUGH MY OWN experiences, I've found that results are directly associated with how I approach successes, as well as how I view challenges. Anyone who has been in business for any length of time is aware of how attitudes can affect productivity and results. Our thoughts and behaviors will determine whether or not we reach our goals.

Much of our work ethic is learned from the time we are children. If we are taught to take joy in our work and the resulting accomplishments, then we learn to enjoy the task and the journey. When we enter the workforce, many people limit themselves to what they believe they can do or what they think they can learn. I'm sure you have employees who think this way. What if you could get your entire organization to change their approach? What if you could lead them into a better frame of mind?

Your company is a reflection of your leadership and direction. While having a positive mental attitude may not be all it takes for a business to be financially successful, a positive outlook certainly makes it easier to reach your goals. I'm not talking about sitting around the conference table thinking good thoughts. I'm talking about engaging in actions that reflect a positive mental outlook.

For instance, I spent years in sales and marketing. My attitudes set the template for whether I succeeded or not. If my sales were down, the decrease could have been caused by my own fears. Those same fears can keep anyone from attaining success. Some of us actually fear success more than we fear failure.

Studies surrounding success and failure show that there is a fluctuation in productivity. These studies not only apply to people in sales, but also in areas of business productivity. When sales fall below a predetermined amount, the employee feels a sense of failure so their productivity goes up. This puts them into an area that is their comfort zone. They are most comfortable working at different levels within this zone.

Have you ever noticed that people who are offered a reward for extending themselves will get out of their box and exceed the expectations set for them? They receive a top sales award or get top performance recognition. Many times, the next month their sales drop. Why? The fear of success keeps them where they are. They can't get past that point without feeling discomfort and wanting to return to what feels good.

> *"To the degree we're not living our dreams; our comfort zone has more control of us than we have over ourselves."*
> **--Peter McWilliams**

HOW OFTEN DO you experience your sales falling below a predetermined amount? In Maxwell Maltz's book entitled Psycho Cybernetics, he states that we all automatically adjust our performance to our self-image, just like the auto-pilot mechanism in an airplane will adjust if some turbulence should move it off course. For instance, let's say there is a sales representative who routinely sells $2,000,000 of products a year. One month, this person could bring in a big sale worth $500,000. However, what will happen in the subsequent months after this great effort? Their performance will drop until they are back in alignment with the cybernetic setting.

Although many people will talk about fear of failure or fear of success, I'd like go a step further. In my opinion, individuals automatically sync with their self-image. This is as true with a student's grades as it is with a person struggling with their weight. Yes, people are stuck. They are conditioned to do what they do, just like a thermostat that is set at seventy-two degrees. It may vary one or two degrees, but it will quickly resynchronize itself.

I've learned that there are simple, effective ways to get "unstuck." First, however, you must have the understanding to know where you are currently. Then, you have to make a decision to change. These steps need to be closely and constantly followed by persistent behaviors.

In his famous text Walden, Henry David Thoreau writes, "The mass of men live lives of quiet desperation." Though Thoreau was writing in the mid-nineteenth century, the same truth applies today. Look at how many people are walking around afraid to make mistakes and think that by doing nothing, they can avoid making them. Meanwhile, they are making the biggest mistake possible. It has been said that the greatest risk in life is the one not taken. Indeed, by not making any decision or movement in the direction of a goal, people miss out on the full joy of life. Life isn't about taking the safest route, never taking any risks. Life is meant to be lived, enjoyed, and should reflect the fullest expression of ourselves.

Certainly, we've all experienced failures or shortcomings since we were children. Failure is normal! Unfortunately, too many of us didn't have anyone to instruct us with the lesson that we had not failed as long as we kept moving toward our goals. Instead, from the time we are children, we were allowed, even perhaps encouraged, to give up on our goals as soon as we experienced our first failure. But there's a better way! Failure doesn't have to be permanent. Instead of quitting, take the lesson from the "failures" and learn how to perform better the next time.

Now that we work in the business world, we carry those old experiences with us as "mental tapes" that play over and over in our minds. These mental tapes often reinforce negative thoughts we have about ourselves, or negative things people have told us. These tapes can be devastating. In this book and in my seminars, I address how to handle these old tapes and exchange them for positive messages. As much as we may have gotten away from the conditions and people that are negative, we still have to change the way we think, as a person and as a leader. What goes on mentally manifests itself outwardly in both yourself and your business.

I know, you're probably thinking that you've heard this all before. However, I'd like to share some more advanced concepts with you that find their roots in this familiar circumstance. We can change the outcome in our lives by changing our own decisions and our own thoughts. We can become more effective in making changes if we know the underlying workings that govern our lives. My goal is to assist you and your organization in this process.

First, we begin with dreams of what we want our company to look like in five years or ten years. The more we think about our dreams, the more they become our heart's desire. Remember how you felt when you first started to climb the corporate or professional ladder? You had to believe in yourself. Now as high-level management, you're at what looks like the top of the ladder, but you are only at the top of this ladder. There is a new ladder that rests on all your expertise and knowledge, and this ladder takes you higher than you could go otherwise.

Professionals tend to think that they've peaked when they reach the level of CEO or manager, that they've made it up the corporate ladder to ultimate success and financial security. Some people think that they are sitting on the top of the mountain and that there is only one way to go if they don't stay at the top of their game. They dread the downhill trip, or try to get out while things are good and take an early retirement.

I realize that early retirement sounds pretty good some days, but aren't there some challenges you'd like to take on before you end your career? As for myself, I'm not sure I will ever retire. There are too many exciting things going on in life and too many opportunities available.

What if you could change your occupation or add to its success and be even more effective in your leadership role? What if you could learn a better way of using your leadership skills? And what if these things could increase your wealth in the process?

When you approach your executive team, each member is looking to you for direction. They are accomplished business men and women, but you are the one who is going to show them leadership. They reflect your attitudes.

Here's a great example of a positive attitude: No matter what he hears from others, Paul Hutsey's response is always, "That's great." Hutsey may not agree with everything he hears, but his response is still the same. He chooses to look for what is great about it. He may not use every idea in managing his business, but he is willing to listen, and he keeps his positive attitude in place. He looks for the gem in the middle of the stack of ideas and uses that one without killing the creativity of the others who have offered input. His ability to listen and respond positively seems like a little thing, but it makes a huge difference in how his people respond to him and the organization.

Paul is retired from Prudential Insurance. Using the principles that he learned from Bob Proctor, he took his branch office that was located in a town of 17,500 people, with half of them below the poverty line, from 167th in productivity and sales to the number one Prudential branch. He maintained this position until his retirement. Now, Paul graciously assists in the certification program of LifeSuccess Consultants.

Each person needs to feel that they have a part in the decision. That's what you want. If there is buy-in on the part of the members of your organization, then changes meet far less resistance than those that are handed down through a memo without any regard as to the long-term effects of how employees will respond or not respond. My friend Paul is able to sidestep some of the problems that most organizations go through. Why do we tend to build up more resistance to change than we need to? In my executive coaching business, I've learned that it's not that leaders don't care; it's that they are focused only on the end results.

I believe leaders need to know the "why" for each employee, the "why" for customers, and the "why" for their direction. By addressing these, you become a stronger leader. After all, you want to move your company and your people to the next level. Don't get stuck with the "how" until you know why. You may be scratching your head and wondering what I'm talking about. Remember that earlier in the chapter, we talked about having an open mind for new concepts, new ways of looking at things. This is one of those concepts.

I'm sure you have either been around small children of your own or someone else's. Have you noticed how often they ask "why?" They ask it about everything. Young children want to know why things work, why we do things, and why we don't do things. It is never-ending. As we get older we stop asking that question, but I believe we need to go back to that basic question. When we find the answers to the "whys," we can move on to bigger things.

Now, fast forward to your professional life as a CEO or manager. One of the keys to organizational success is finding out what drives your employees. For now, we are looking at them and not you. What motivates them has a bottom line effect on you and your business as a whole. This means getting to know people who work with you and for you. If you are a large organization, it may be that some of this will be accomplished through your Human Resources Director and their office staff. However, it is important to find out the "why," the reason people do things. Dealing with what drives other people to action can be complex. These questions and others can be addressed in my seminars. Here are some starting places:

What is it that they really want?

What is their heart's desire?

What's going on in their heart of hearts?

As you consider the answers to these questions, you need to consider certain aspects of their life, some of which may be a surprise to you. There are four areas of their lives that you want to examine:

CAREER

FIND OUT WHAT their "why" for their career is. Do they work at their job because they are convinced they can't do anything else? Do they simply work in a J-O-B, or is their position a career step in a long ladder of success? Is this their dream job? What keeps them coming to work? Do they get to use their skills and develop new ones? These questions are just a start.

RELATIONSHIPS

IN ADDITION, YOU want to find out what is their "why" in their marriage or long-term relationships with significant others. What about their other key relationships with their kids, loved ones, and friends? You want to find out what is their "why" as it pertains to their growth financially. In psychologist Abraham Maslow's studies, he began with the basic needs of individuals. The first "why" on his hierarchy of needs is meeting those essential needs to maintain life. We need shelter, food, clothing, transportation, and a way to retain them. That is the first "why" of your employees. When those basic needs are met, then you can move on to other levels of need and wants.

I must warn you here that most employees are not thinking of the company first. As a manager, you probably are thinking of the company first because it is "your baby." For lower-level employees, however, after they meet personal needs of survival, they are most concerned about their families. That's what matters to them.

HEALTH

FIND OUT WHAT their "why" is with the health of their physical body. Are they distracted with personal illnesses or chronic issues that affect your bottom line as well? Are they in good health? Do they have a healthy mental outlook?

FINANCES

THE "WHY" THAT concerns people most often is how they are going to pay for the necessities of life. After that is accomplished, most people have things that they want for themselves or their family. Do they feel like they are being paid what they are worth? Are they frustrated working for someone else? Would they like to be doing something else for more money? Are they satisfied with their financial status?

We will examine all four of these areas together and work to find out the answers. When you've unlocked the "whys" for your employees, you will unlock some of the areas you haven't been able to get to and become more efficient. Connect them to their "why." In the process you'll find out, as I have, that knowing the "whys" will always move people beyond where they think that they can go. Always!

In my experience, I've learned that people who understand why they are motivated and what motivates them as they explore the "why" within their employees and themselves become more committed to their goals. After examining the "whys," let's examine the possible outcomes that you face in your organization and how they are different than the results you truly want to accomplish. Within the constellation of your interests, you face many factors. Daily operations include the following:

Concerns over capital available for expansion

Development of new products

Asset management

Dealing with customers and suppliers

Scheduling for challenges that may be out of your immediate
control but affect your bottom line

Structural issues in your line of authority

Communications

Productivity

THE LIST GOES on and on. In this era of constant and immediate information exchange, you may still find problems with getting hardware to work correctly and make the information you need available exactly when you need it. Maybe you have software issues, or you are in need of revamping your computer tech's policy on handling upkeep and repairs, as well as meeting the growing needs of new programs and developing systems that work best for your type of business.

Whether they are customers, suppliers or employees, dealing with other people takes up a large amount of energy. Many organizations have a Human Resources department to take care of those inner-company issues, but what about those forces that impact your business from the outside? Are there bumpy spots in your road? If you are a small company, you may wear many hats.

In working with a client, I address these concerns and more. Like other CEOs, I'm sure you want the environment you have created to be one of maximum creativity, productivity, and accountability. If the expectations of your management are not expressed or integrated into your training of new employees, then the employees don't actually know what is expected of them. How often does your company have job evaluations? Is there any ongoing feedback between supervisors and staff? Unsatisfied expectations are one of the biggest problems that plague businesses and individual people, as well.

Let's stop here and go back to the basics of leadership for a moment. The basic concept of leadership is something we learned about in school and is defined in many ways. Of course, being a leader doesn't mean that you are just in a particular position in an office. Leadership involves a person's ability to guide others and give them direction. In addition, we say that leaders have the abilities to show the way to others. Some people think they are natural leaders, but when they turn around and look behind them, they don't see anyone following. Others seem to naturally attract a following.

I believe that whether you are a natural or a trained leader, I can help you to be even better. You can become more effective at taking initiative. I have worked with professionals to develop their skills and continue as a coach.

You already know that the leadership skills you practice organizationally are an exercise in your ability to influence and motivate others to contribute to the success of your organization as a team and as individuals. How you lead directly impacts the professionalism practiced in your offices. Your leadership style makes a difference in your earnings, satisfaction, and how effectively your share is in the market place for your products or services. Your organization probably reflects your strengths as well as those things you find challenging.

Different leadership styles affect how your employees and customers see you and your organization. We're going to examine these different styles.

AUTHORITARIAN

IN THE AUTHORITARIAN or autocratic style, the activities of your entire organization are directed from one source. Usually in that case, there is very little feedback coming up the ladder. The leader may be operating in a vacuum and not even realize it. From their viewpoint, things appear to be running smoothly as long as the corporate earnings are good and employees are doing what they are told. This type of leader is results-oriented. Those who are down the organizational chart from them may not realize that. In some circumstances, this style is needed for quick decision-making. However, some such leaders can become micromanagers and unintentionally kill the motivation to perform well as an employee. They may be seen as abusive or difficult to get along with.

DEMOCRATIC

THE PARTICIPATIVE OR democratic style is one that involves other people in decision-making. Leadership is usually associated with one person, but as you also know, leadership can be the core group at the top of the organization who work directly with the CEO. When other employees have a part of the information, they share the responsibility for the wellbeing of the organization and are part of the process. Participating with your employees reinforces the cooperative atmosphere of the organization. Leading by example with hands-on work when everyone needs to pitch in can be found in this style.

DELEGATION

THIS STYLE OF leadership entails giving your employees free reign to use their knowledge and skills to accomplish the organization's business goals. Delegation doesn't pass the responsibility fully on to the employees. The buck still stops with the CEO, ultimately. Accountability must work at all levels for this style to be at its best.

The best leaders are those who can be flexible using all of these styles as needed by circumstances or the daily routine of conducting business. In a seminar or in coaching, we work together to identify your most common style, the one you spend most of your time in. Then, I will help you learn to flex in and out of each style as needed to be a more successful leader.

One aspect of leadership that I come across fairly often in my coaching and seminars is that of leaders having unmet expectations or unrealistic expectations of their employees. This pitfall can cause one of your biggest headaches and can cause the most damage in employee-management relations. New leaders are not the only ones that must safeguard against this potential downfall. Clarity in how you communicate and reflect expectations is important to maintain. We will discuss communications in a later chapter.

Even though you have a long track record of decision-making, you may occasionally doubt a decision that resulted in dissatisfaction from your employees or your customers. You used the best information you had at the time to make that choice, but the outcome didn't meet your expectations. Maybe your sales dropped for the last quarter because of discontinuing a product that appeared to be losing its appeal. However, the new improved item or a replacement item was not received well. An example that still resonates in people's minds was when Coca Cola™ changed their formula in 1985. The new product was unofficially called "New Coke" and was expected to capture the new "flavor" of the nineteen-eighties, but by and large, the public hated the taste of it. Coca-Cola had to reintroduce the original flavor, and this time, the company's marketing presented consumers with "Classic Coke™." Once again, the customers were happy.

The CEO of Coca Cola probably doubted his decision-making abilities for at least a little while. It happens to many executives. Dwelling on your past mistakes, instead of learning the lesson and moving on to the next product can be detrimental to your future. In my experience, it's normal to feel doubt sometimes, but I've learned that we don't have to dwell there. We can choose to look for the positive actions and decisions and focus on success instead of failure.

A poem I like is a great example of how our mindset affects us in the way we fill our positions of leadership:

One ship sails East,
And another West,
By the self-same winds that blow,
Tis the set of the sails
And not the gales,
That tells the way we go.
Like the winds of the sea
Are the waves of time,
As we journey along through life,
Tis the set of the soul,
That determines the goal,
And not the calm or the strife.
-- Ella Wheeler Wilcox

ANOTHER ASPECT OF leadership we can examine together is whether you made a conscious choice to be where you are today, or if the path you started out on has somehow changed over time. Did you end up someplace that you weren't planning on going, but now you are there and aren't sure how you got off track? We can examine that together and make a course correction if that's what is needed.

In my own life, I'm on a different path than the one I chose when I started working in the professional world. In the years I spent in marketing, I learned many valuable lessons that have helped me as a professional coach. "Marketing and innovation are the two chief functions of business. You get paid for creating a customer, which is marketing. And you get paid for creating a new dimension of performance, which is innovation. Everything else is a cost center."

PETER DRUCKER

IN THIS BOOK, I want to appeal to your innovation as a leader. There isn't one leadership personality. Just like ice cream, leaders come in many flavors. Individual temperaments influence your effectiveness with others. I'm sure you will agree that as a CEO or top-level manager, you deal with people as much as you do with products and procedures. If you locked in on procedures at the exclusion of other factors, your employees and customers may think you don't care about them. I've found that a balance of focus on people, products, and procedures works well. Then, I combine them with natural laws and concepts that have made me successful, and I share that with my clients. I want you to see a snapshot of some business leaders that I most admire.

MARY KAY ASH

MARY KAY ASH was born in a small town, Hot Wells, Texas in 1918 and grew up to be a U.S. businesswoman and the founder of Mary Kay Cosmetics, Inc. She worked in direct sales companies from the 1930s until the early 1960s. Ash achieved considerable success as a salesperson and trainer. Frustrated at being passed over for promotions in favor of men, she retired in 1963.

Mary Kay intended to write a how-to book to assist business women in building success. The book turned into a business plan and in September 1963, Ash and her son, Richard Rogers, began Mary Kay Cosmetics with a $5,000 investment. The company originally started in a storefront in Dallas but grew rapidly. The famous pink Cadillacs awarded to top sales people in her cosmetic company were the most visible sign of the company's success.

Ash was widely respected for her approach to business. She considered the Golden Rule the founding principle of Mary Kay Cosmetics. Her marketing plan was designed to allow women to advance by helping others to succeed. She was supportive and enthusiastic. Mary Kay thought you should "praise people to success." Her slogan "God first, family second, career third" showed her priority that the women in her company keep all aspects of their lives in balance.

JACK CANFIELD

ONE OF THE men who I really admire is Jack Canfield. Most people know him as the co-creator, along with Mark Victor Hansen, of the #1 New York Times bestselling Chicken Soup book series. However, you may not know that Canfield is also a professional motivational speaker on the subjects of self-esteem, performance, professional development and the psychology behind success, as well as being a corporate trainer and coach. I offer you the same principles that Jack Canfield teaches as a success coach and corporate trainer. Like him, I've learned how to use these concepts for success.

Jack Canfield says, "The problem is the average person isn't tuned in to lifelong learning, or going to seminars and so forth. If the information is not on television, and it's not in the movies they watch, and it's not in the few books that they buy, they don't get it." I agree with him. Many people who are in leadership roles have stopped learning and don't understand why their wealth and success has peaked. Learning is a process that should never stop. I learned that myself several years ago when I became frustrated with the corporate world and my level of success in it. I wanted more and I found a way to obtain the things I wanted. It started with studying and listening to others who had keys to open the places I hadn't been able to reach. Constantly involving myself in continuing-education programs has opened many doors for me. Just because you have earned a degree and are working in high-level management, don't assume you have nothing else to learn!

Self-development and a willingness to learn new things are traits that a good leader maintains. Training employees is an important part of conducting a prosperous business, yet some CEOs forget that they need to feed themselves as well. From working with CEOs in the past, I've learned that most of you are committed, determined, focused, and are risk-takers. That's how you reached your position. I want to assist you and reinforce those qualities. Part of your willingness to be a risk-taker is your willingness to spend money in order to achieve goals. There is a very old saying, "You have to spend money to make money." That is true. Don't get stuck in the mindset that you have to wait to have the resources before you can do anything.

As a leader you can make decisions to achieve goals, and then the money needed will be provided. Don't let yourself be limited by the mindset of thinking about what you lack instead of what you can become. Combining your knowledge and experience with concepts that Jack Canfield and I use everyday can be exactly what is missing in your strategy.

BOB PROCTOR

I GREATLY ADMIRE Bob Proctor. He has studied the psychology and natural laws of success for over four decades. He did not grow up in a rich family. In his twenties, his was a firefighter and decided he wanted more out of life than that. Bob wanted to be successful and wealthy. He quit his job and made his dream of wealth come true. He learned practical concepts that worked for him and can work for anyone, no matter where they are.

Bob Proctor learned success concepts from Earl Nightingale. These same principles go back to Napoleon Hill's book, Think and Grow Rich. It was the first of a classification of books that inspired people to better their circumstances. Hill was inspired by Andrew Carnegie, who shared his secrets for success and wealth. I am excited to know that what I practice in business and share with my clients has a direct line to that source. I am a part of the Bob Proctor Coaching Program and have become better at what I offer to my clients because of it. One of my favorite quotes from Bob is, "When you really want something, and you couple that with an understanding of your nature, of your spiritual being, and the laws that govern you, you will keep going, regardless of what's happened. Nothing will stop you."

DONALD TRUMP

TRUMP IS ANOTHER on my list of people who I admire. He is one of the richest, most successful men of our time. A Baby Boomer, his wealthy father made his money in real estate in New York. Even more successful than his father, Trump has made billions in real estate and the entertainment industry, including casinos. But not everything has always gone well for him, though. In the early 1990's, he had to file Chapter 11 Bankruptcy professionally, not personally. However, he has written several successful books on business and getting rich. He has also come out of his financial challenges and is one of the most recognizable business men in the world.

There are several quotes from Donald Trump that I like, but this one is one of my favorites. It shows something about why he has been as successful as he is. Trump said, "Part of being a winner is knowing when enough is enough. Sometimes you have to give up the fight and walk away, and move on to something that's more productive." That statement inspires me to be open to ideas and concepts that can improve my life.

WARREN BUFFET

ANOTHER SUCCESSFUL BUSINESS leader I admire is Warren Buffet. Known as an American investor, a highly successful businessman, and a generous philanthropist, Buffet is the third richest person in the world according to Forbes magazine. Buffet's leadership and savvy business decisions have made him admirable. He still lives in the same house he bought years ago in Omaha, but he enjoys the life he chose. To me, one of his most admirable qualities is that of maintaining his wealth while helping others and making the world a better place because of his generosity.

Buffet once said, "The business schools reward difficult, complex behavior more than simple behavior, but simple behavior is more effective." The concepts in this book and my seminars are not complicated; they are simply missed in our formal educations and business schools. When I began using them in my life on a daily basis, the success I truly wanted was within my reach.

MICHAEL GERBER

MICHAEL GERBER IS also an amazing example of success. He is a leader in small business. Author of The E-Myth Revisited: Why Most Small Businesses Don't Work And What To Do About It, Gerber has left his mark on the business world. In the book, he addresses the "daily grind" of work that seems to kill creativity and innovation. His philosophies speak to some of the factors we will discuss in this book. Gerber speaks to audiences internationally about bringing joy and satisfaction into the corporate world for a more satisfying life. Michael Gerber is quoted as saying, "The difference between great people and everyone else is that great people create their lives actively, while everyone else is created by their lives, passively waiting to see where life takes them next. The difference between the two is the difference between living fully and just existing."

Another Gerber quote that I believe to be of great guidance for entrepreneurs (and one I would be remiss if I left out) is, "The entrepreneur is our visionary, the creator in each of us. We're born with that quality and it defines our lives as we respond to what we see, hear, feel, and experience. It is developed, nurtured, and given space to flourish, or is squelched, thwarted, without air or stimulation, and dies."

BILL GATES

I ADMIRE BILL Gates. He created a corporation and professional reputation that is known worldwide. His name is a household word. His leadership in business and his technological innovation touch every one of us, wherever we live. He is admired by many for his innovations in developing the computer revolution. His technology's impact on business and our private lives has been amazing.

Gates started Microsoft with Paul Allen. Even though some have criticized his business practices concerning competition, he is still recognized as an icon in American business. Bill Gates knew what he wanted to do and never allowed limitations to hinder his progress. His focus and resolve to accomplish his goals are exemplary to all of us.

Bill Gates is also known for his philanthropic activities. He and his wife began the Bill and Melinda Gates Foundation. One of their greatest concerns is education and what they can do to make a difference. He has been influenced greatly by Warren Buffet to focus on helping others. His success has given him the abundance resulting from a focused mind and concerted effort. As other business and corporate leaders have done, he deliberately worked toward his specific goals and he accomplished what he set out to do.

Bill Gates said, "I'm a great believer that any tool that enhances communication has profound effects in terms of how people can learn from each other, and how they can achieve the kind of freedoms that they're interested in."

Although there are other successful leaders in the corporate world, these are some great examples of what leadership can accomplish. I've found that studying these successful entrepreneurs in addition to my experience makes me a better facilitator and trainer for organizations and professionals.

LEADERSHIP EXERCISE

WE HAVE BRIEFLY looked at what leadership means and examined its different styles. We've looked at examples of outstanding business leaders. In preparation for using this book and my services, take a few minutes to think about the following questions and jot down your thoughts. This is your first step in beginning our walk together.

What style of leadership am I most comfortable using? _____

_____

_____

_____

_____

_____

_____

_____

*What style is a reach for me?*_____

_____

_____

_____

_____

_____

_____

_____

*What areas of leadership are my strengths?q*_____

_____

_____

_____

_____

_____

_____

_____

_____

*What areas of leadership are most challenging to me?*_____

_____

_____

_____

_____

_____

_____

_____

_____

POINTS TO REMEMBER

- Thoughts affect attitude, and attitude affects behavior.
- Your organization is a reflection of your leadership and direction.
- Your approach makes a difference in the bottom line results.
- Fear can hinder success.
- There is more success and wealth available to you through using universal concepts than you may have thought.
- Learn the "why" of those people around you and then learn your own.
- Know your leadership style, whether it is authoritarian, democratic, or delegating. The best leaders flex between all three.
- Your mindset affects your success level.
- Through my seminars we can put all these pieces together to make you a stronger and more successful leader.

Chapter Two

PROFESSIONAL SUCCESS

Chapter Two

PROFESSIONAL SUCCESS

"Your purpose explains what you are doing with your life. Your vision explains how you are living your purpose. Your goals enable you to realize your vision."
-- **Bob Proctor**

THE RELATIONSHIP BETWEEN purpose and vision affects whether or not we reach our goals. Each one of us has a purpose that is distinctly ours. The line of business that we have chosen should reflect that. Most of us try to find our dream job when we start out our careers. Others settle for what they can get until they find something better. In the same way that you've found a successful career, you've followed a path that began with thoughts as to what you believed your purpose to be. Then, you moved on to the vision of what life could be professionally and personally. Finally, you reached the goals that you set out to accomplish, or you may still be on that path to accomplishment.

Are there areas of your business that represent challenges to you, where the goals seem elusive? I believe that I can assist you in targeting and attaining those goals. This book introduces the basics of the tools I work with in organizational seminars as a consultant.

How far would you get on a journey if you didn't have an itinerary or plan? If you are going somewhere you've never been, you need a roadmap to follow. Otherwise, you could end up in a place you don't want to be or get stuck on a long detour that saps your resources. That can happen in your business and keep you from achieving the results you want.

Many people in the United States use MapQuest™ to get directions from where they are to where they want to go. The key to using it for the best results is to know where you are starting from and where you want to end up at the end of the trip. Setting goals that are really exciting and inspiring can be just the incentive to get us heading down the road.

I like one of the analogies that Bob Proctor uses. Imagine you're dropping down from the sky with a parachute. You have a map stuffed in your pocket. Your destination is Denver, Colorado. However, if you don't know where you have landed, you may end up somewhere you hadn't planned on being. This is where we need to do an honest appraisal of our strengths and weaknesses, and start looking for what we need to do so that we can achieve our goal for true success.

I've been on road trips where the map didn't reflect current reality. I had to reassess my plan and adjust my directions in order to get to my destination. It's like taking a trip across the ocean on a ship. Each day, the actual location is confirmed. If they need to make a course adjustment in order to stay on the right track to get to their destination, they will make that correction.

The concepts we are discussing briefly in this book are those that you receive in depth in my seminars and coaching. Some may not be new ideas, but they are probably things that you know unconsciously. We will examine ways to use those concepts into your daily life so you can be even more successful than you already are. If you're still making course adjustments in order to achieve your goals, I think that this book will make your life richer and more satisfying. Whatever stage your career is at currently, whether it is a manager or the CEO of your organization, you can be more than you are today. Rather than trying to navigate your course the old-fashioned way, come with me and let me open the way to global positioning that will give you a huge payoff.

*"What a different story people would have to tell if they would adopt
a definite purpose and stand by that purpose
until it had time to become an all-consuming purpose."*
--Napoleon Hill, from Laws of Success

NOT HAVING A purpose is like being caught out at sea without a compass or a sextant. How do you find the way to your destination? I have found that we don't just drift through life without picking up skills and finding out what we really enjoy doing. Finding those things that we are naturally good at isn't an accident. That is part of why we are here on Earth, to discover what our unique gifts are and then use them. We don't all have the same talents and gifts. Each person has a distinctive set that is theirs alone. Yours may be similar to someone else's, but no one has the exact combination that you were given.

You and I found our purpose by experimenting and working at different jobs or careers until we found the one that we could really identify with. If you're still not sure you've found yours, then we can also discover that on this journey together.

If you are working in a profession where you make good money but aren't happy doing it, maybe you should take another look at what your purpose really is. You may be talented and enjoy something that you wanted to major in at college or that you worked at early in your twenties. Then someone came along and told you that your choice was interesting to study, but you could never make money at it. I've found, as have many others, that statement isn't true. They wanted you to agree with them and do something else that they wanted for you, but let me repeat, it isn't true. The fact is, you can make money at anything that you love.

Ella Williams said, "Bite off more than you can chew, then chew it." The point I'm trying to make is that part of leadership and developing your own professionalism is finding and knowing your purpose. Then you can see a vision of what life can be, and you can set goals in order to reach success. We will discuss goals and achieving them in more detail later in the book.

One of the errors I've come across with some of my clients is the mistake of thinking that activity and motion are supposed to equal action. If you and your employees are stuck in what seems to be many time-consuming activities, then you are in a trap. Success is not about making work where there isn't any actual work. And success is certainly not about shuffling though and processing reams of paperwork with no measurable result or increased income.

Professionalism involves actual accomplishment and the way in which you conduct your business. A person rushing around in apparent crisis mode over small issues is distracting to actual business. If there is a real crisis that must be handled, then people should stop, handle the crisis or solve the problem, and then go back to what they were doing. If your purpose is to manufacture widgets, then that is your focus. Don't get distracted by things that don't matter.

In Gerry Robert's book The Millionaire Mindset, he states several affirmations that he calls "money magnets." The one that I think fits perfectly with exploring professionalism is the sixth affirmation: "I am a master of massive action. I am very active. I enjoy making things happen. Things seem to fall into place for me! Money comes my way because of my positive habits and actions. I know what questions to ask to generate solutions, and I act immediately on the answers I get." As a consultant, I've learned that this is a great way to describe your business day; it is the result of your professionalism.

If you haven't used affirmations before, this may sound a little strange to you, but they are an active way of exercising your positive thinking for results. The power of affirmations and visualizations can make an amazing difference in your life and your success level. Seeing your goals as already accomplished is a first step to making them happen.

The general public describes professionalism as dressing in a gray suit, white shirt, and a conservative striped tie. Shoes are highly polished, and you have the proper short haircut. If you are a woman, you wear a black or navy two-piece suit and conservative pumps. Your hair is done perfectly, you have impeccable makeup and professionally manicured nails.

Professionals carry a laptop computer bag or a leather briefcase. They eat in the right places, attend important board or executive meetings, and hold one-on-one appointments with highly successful and influential people. They have a business degree, most likely an MBA.

This is the general public's description of what a professional looks like. I believe there is more to it than what you look like on the outside and what activities are found on your calendar. Professionalism begins on the inside. The business leaders listed in Chapter One have these characteristics, plus persistence and vision.

"Nothing in this world can take the place of persistence.
Talent will not; nothing is more common than unsuccessful people with talent.
Genius will not; unrewarded genius is almost a proverb."
--Calvin Coolidge

I'VE ALSO LEARNED that the path we all follow in professional success is not somewhere we walk alone. Whether we are a one-person company or a business with many employees working with us, we are part of a network. We become stronger when we share the universal concepts used in my seminars. The Bob Proctor LifeSuccess Consultants program that I am part of and use with my own clients is a sharing opportunity that can make a huge difference for you.

It surprises me how many people I meet who want to be more successful than they are currently, but are unsure of how to get from where they are to where they want to be. However, if we aren't aware of things that can help us, we can't use them. That is why it is so important to learn what our purpose is. I've come back to discuss purpose again because I think it acts like the rudder on a boat.

Discovering a more abundant success than you ever thought you could have is exciting and empowering. When I realized this truth, I sat up and took notice of the accomplishments that I had experienced along the path, not just at the top of the mountain. I began to grow personally and professionally. I found it is a process. That's what persistence is all about.

Remember what it was like when you learned to ride a bike or skate on inline skates? You fell down sometimes, but you got back up on your bike and tried again. Your mom or dad probably held on the bicycle seat to help steady you and ran along beside you. Then one day, you realized they were standing behind you somewhere clapping and shouting for joy as they watched you ride on your own. The next time you got on your bicycle, it was easier. Each time your balance was better and you rode farther, until it was like walking. Soon enough, riding a bike felt natural and easy.

What about those inline skates? You had to strengthen your ankles. A friend probably held your arm or hand while you learned to skate. Then, one day you strapped on those skates and went anywhere you wanted. That same experience of teaching others to ride a bike or inline skate is what I do when I'm working with my clients. I help them to strengthen their muscles and learn how to keep their balance until they are successful. Each time I share with someone else, I feel I am one step closer to a better world. We can all be as successful or wealthy as we choose to be.

Just like we learn to be aware of what it takes to maintain our balance on a bike or skates, we can become aware of the universal laws and apply them. Becoming conscious is the first step of our path together. If you stop there, you only have part of the puzzle. To go back to the analogy of learning to ride a bicycle, if you stopped the first time you fell or refused to ride unless your dad held the seat, you only allowed yourself to get the principle of keeping your balance. You never reached the point of actually using it to become a better rider.

What if Lance Armstrong had never learned to ride a bike? What if he had given up in his fight against cancer? At the time of his devastating diagnosis, he was given a very small chance of surviving. But he took that chance! And he came back to be a very successful cyclist, a household name, in fact. Lance didn't accomplish his goals all by himself; he had a team of trainers and riders, but he decided to be a world-class professional road racing cyclist. Before he retired, he won seven Tour de France road races.

The most successful people know what their purpose is and persist in what it takes to realize wealth and success. Our purpose is our determination to act a certain way with intention. That intention can start with only an idea of what we think we want. We act on what we are thinking. As our thoughts persist, we begin to see a clear picture of what it is we want to accomplish or acquire. That vision can start with a concept that began with your thought process. Your imagination may give it substance. You know what you want, what it looks like, and now you can set a goal to reach your dreams.

Conscious awareness during this process is one of the pillars of success. Before the Wright brothers flew for the first time, they had to be aware of the possibilities and then work towards that goal. The brothers used information that was available to them as well as others, but they used thought patterns that built on their awareness.

"You have the freedom to be yourself,
your true self, here and now - and nothing can stand in your way!"
--from Jonathan Livingston Seagull

PART OF WHAT we are talking about in this book is a new way of thinking about the world and our place in it. We live in an abundant world. Why then do some people suffer and barely have enough to survive? It's actually not just circumstances. We can change the way our lives are lived and be able to share in the abundance that is around us. Our universe has more galaxies and stars than we can count. There are more grains of sand on the beach then we can count. Every plant on earth produces seeds or nuts that make it possible for us to have more plants. Animals, fish, and birds multiply. Nothing is finite.

Why do we spend so much time thinking that there isn't enough money or things for us to have what we want? As children, we learned a whole list of things that we took as true. Bob Proctor calls these thoughts a poverty mindset. We could list pages and pages of these statements we've heard our whole lives, but I want you to read through only some of them so that you can focus on an important truth: these statements are simply someone's opinion that they are trying to enforce on you. They are not true facts, and you don't have to believe them anymore!

Money doesn't grow on trees.
We can't afford to do that; it is for rich people.
Don't get your hopes up.
You can try, but don't expect to win.
Be realistic.
Stop dreaming.
Get your head out of the clouds and be practical.
You'll never achieve that.
It costs too much.
You have to be lucky to get that.
Save your pennies.

BE CAREFUL.

I'M SURE YOU have heard these and other statements over and over again from family, friends, and associates. Let me remind you, these are not true. Your professional success is up to you. I can assist you in ways to make your purpose, vision, and goals become your reality.

Where did we get the idea that it was somehow "bad" to be wealthy and have the things we want for ourselves and our families? Being poor is not a virtue. Likewise, being wealthy is not a sin. People like Bill Gates, Donald Trump, Bob Proctor, Oprah Winfrey, and others enjoy their wealth, but also do things for others. They chose to help the world be a better place. There are plenty of successful and wealthy people who enjoy their lives and are happy. Many people say wealth is only a tool. Then why not use it and make it work for you?

I've learned that money doesn't make you happy. The pursuit of money isn't supposed to be your source of happiness. However, I believe that money is supposed to do two things. First, money provides you with things so you are comfortable. Second, money enables you to make a difference beyond your physical presence.

When someone is too focused on their basic needs, they are not helping anyone else in the process of "being, doing, or having." People who have more than they need for the basics are able to contribute towards causes and other's needs. Many people do what they can for others, but are unable to do much because of financial concerns. They are not making a significant contribution to the world. Making world changes takes money. The more you make, the more you can do for others and make a better world to live in.

Don't misunderstand me. I'm not saying there is some magical way for you to be professionally successful without any effort, but I am saying that your state of mind is a factor. I'm also not saying that you won't have any obstacles to get over. You can choose to look at them as something that limits you and keeps your from progressing toward your goal, or you can choose to see opportunities in your path. Only you can decide. If you learn to take the lessons from each challenge and put them in your tool box, you will get past the same obstacle the next time it gets in your way more quickly. I've worked with professionals on these aspects of facing stumbling blocks, and they have learned to take lessons from the experience.

"Tough times never last, but tough people do."
--Robert Schuller

MY SEMINARS HELP you learn that you're not alone. All of us need to learn how to tap into our inner selves and apply lessons to our problems. Everyone has problems of one kind or another. None of us go through life without ever encountering obstacles. Sometimes we get stuck thinking that we don't want to make a mistake. We fear that our obstacles could ruin our professional reputation or our career. But it's a mistake to think that denying your problems is the best course of action! If you don't do something about them, if you don't take action, you're going to lose out on what could have been. How many people later in life look back and wish they had done things differently? If we don't do something, we won't accomplish anything.

If what you are doing to solve your problems isn't working, it may be that you need to do something different. Don't be afraid to learn new viewpoints and try other ways of looking at your problem. We can fall into old habits that keep us from progressing on the path to true success. Those things that keep you from moving on should be discarded. Replace them with something that does work. Twenty-one days are all that's required to change a habit. Imagine if you created a new habit that would make you more successful each month of the year.

It is a matter of practicing discipline. Like the habits you are working on, discipline will become stronger the more you use it. Exercise it like a muscle and it will develop. Think about whom some of your role models are in business. I shared some of mine with you, but think about what it is they do that makes them successful. I literally did that when I started the path I'm on as a consultant with Bob Proctor's LifeSuccess Consulting program. What a difference this program made in my success level! That is what I want to share with you so that you, too, can realize the elusive goals that you think about but haven't achieved yet.

I've learned that changing the way you think actually changes your results. Real, permanent change begins with desire. Most of us think of change as a wish, but I think it is more than that. It is a longing for something, but it also indicates a strong intention or purpose. See how it ties together? We cover this and more in my seminars.

Napoleon Hill's book Think & Grow Rich has a chapter about desire. In it he says, "There is one quality one must possess to win, and that is definiteness of purpose, the knowledge of what one wants, and a burning desire to possess it." Desire is the unexpressed possibility within a person seeking expression outside the person.

Faith is a part of this path, also. Faith is closely tied to purpose, vision, and goals. It is literally knowing or believing something is real that you can't actually see or touch. This complete trust in something that you can't see is found in religions as well as universal laws. Faith usually has strong conviction. Those of us who have studied and applied the concepts found in The Secret are convinced that these universal laws are there for anyone to use. We just have to make that decision.

In another chapter from Think & Grow Rich, Hill begins by saying, "Faith is the head chemist of the mind." When writing his book, he very carefully chose each word to get the message that he wanted across to his readers. I've found in reading it myself that I could spend hours just contemplating what each sentence tells me.

Another part of this path that I include in my seminars is the "attitude of gratitude." It may be well known to many of us, but how many of us practice it on a daily basis in our private and professional lives? A huge difference will be made if you incorporate it into the way you act and talk with your business associates and employees. Gratitude for others makes them feel good about themselves, but you also receive a blessing when you appreciate others. Think of how you respond to appreciation from others for a job well done. They also respond to that same feeling. Gratitude gives you a more positive outlook when you apply it to the things around you.

Having gratitude and expressing it in all areas is a major step in experiencing a balanced life filled with meaning. What is it that ignites your passion? What are the first things you think of each morning and the last thing every night? What would you rather do than eat or sleep? That is your passion. Pursue it! Take the steps you need in order to make a decision about what you want. Then you have to believe with your heart and mind that you can achieve it. Remember that it begins with your state of mind, and take action every day to realize your goal. I believe that a primary key to unlocking abundance is being eternally grateful for all of the blessings in your life.

Once you've put a plan into action for your success along with practicing persistence and determination, you will see the results. I've found in my experience that all the resources and opportunities I need present themselves when the time is right. If you stay focused on finding them, opportunities will direct you to the next step on the way to reaching your goals and achieving the results you want.

One of my favorite quotes about purpose and the place it has in our personal and professional success is by John William Gardner. Gardner was born in Los Angeles, California, in 1912, and after a long and successful life he died in 2002. He is known for writing Excellence: Can We Be Equal and Excellent Too? (1961), Self-Renewal: The Individual and the Innovative Society (1964), and No Easy Victories (1968).

> *"Some people have greatness thrust upon them. Few have excellence thrust upon them; they achieve it. They do not achieve it unwittingly by doing what comes naturally and they don't stumble into it in the course of amusing themselves. All excellence involves discipline and tenacity of purpose."*
> -- **John William Gardner**

LEADERSHIP EXERCISE

THE FOLLOWING QUESTIONS will help you continue preparing for our further exploration of your success. Like the previous exercise in Chapter One, these are meant to get you thinking. It helps to have a focus for your seminar that begins with your needs and thoughts. Then as your consultant, I can guide you further down the path.

Do you know what your purpose is professionally? Describe it here: _____

_____

_____

_____

_____

_____

_____

_____

_____

What does your vision look like? _____

_____

_____

_____

_____

_____

_____

_____

_____

_____

Do you practice unproductive activities? What are they? _____

_____

_____

_____

_____

_____

_____

_____

_____

Do you have a positive or limited mindset? _____

_____

_____

_____

_____

_____

_____

_____

POINTS TO REMEMBER

- Your purpose and vision affect whether or not your goals are reached.
- A plan and a direction are part of the course we navigate on our way to success.
- Activity is not a measure of progress.
- Professionalism is a state of mind.
- Persistence is key to success.
- Stay away from limited thinking, your own or someone else's.

Chapter Three

YOUR ORGANIZATION

Chapter Three

YOUR ORGANIZATION

"Every memorable act in the history of the world is a triumph of enthusiasm. Nothing great was ever achieved without it because it gives any challenge or any occupation, no matter how frightening or difficult, a new meaning. Without enthusiasm you are doomed to a life of mediocrity, but with it, you can accomplish miracles."
Og Mandino, 1923-1996, Speaker and Author

EACH ORGANIZATION, WHETHER it is a business or a group who has come together with shared interests, develops a unique culture based on the members of the group. Change one person, and the dynamics of the group will change. Each person sees the world from their own viewpoint shaped by their own experiences, upbringing, education, exposure to new ideas, and belief system. Individual members leave a mark on the group's culture through their thoughts and actions. Sometimes it is as subtle as the silent influence that someone exercises in their organization. You as the CEO are the most influential person, or at least, you should be.

However, if you're having difficulty in reaching some people and getting the results you want, it may be that you are unaware of the roles that others take within that group of people. Learning about those roles can help you see things from a new point of view. Usually, they are exercised informally and unconsciously.

THE INFORMAL LEADER

THERE IS AN "informal" leader who people follow in the day-to-day routines. This person is probably not setting out to circumvent your position or leadership, but he or she inadvertently happen into such roles because he or she connects on a personal and professional basis with those who may not respond as well to your style of communication.

Unless there are legal or ethical reasons to reproach the informal leader, they can be a huge asset to you in getting those elusive results you're after. You want to cultivate their buy-in to what you want to accomplish. Your influence with them will reach into the areas where their influence extends. Others will feel a part of the decision-making and the process of succeeding through that channel.

THE DEVIL'S ADVOCATE

MOST GROUPS HAVE someone who listens to every idea and always finds something wrong with it or thinks it could be done differently. This person is called a "devil's advocate." Sometimes, they may be seen as disruptive during discussions, but they have a valid point that should be considered. This person asks the "what ifs" and "should we do it this way?" Often we tend to put this person off because we think they just like to disagree. In my experience, that isn't always the case. The devil's advocate in your group is a valuable member, and one who is the most circumspect. He or she is considering the same information you are from a different point of view. Often, the devil's advocate can foresee potential problems before anyone else can. As CEO, you can choose to consider this point-of-view along with the opinions from other members of your group or team.

Remember, when we experience differences of opinion or dissention, it is normal. We are not going to agree on everything all of the time. If we let our personal feelings override our professionalism, then it needs to be addressed on a one-on-one basis. I work with clients on how they deal with each other in each circumstance.

THE NOTE TAKER

IN BUSINESS, YOU probably have a secretary or assistant who takes notes in meetings. However, there is usually a member of a group or organization that is a natural record keeper. They jot notes on a pad in every meeting. They keep notes on everything. When you work with them, it's easy to find out details and information that others may have missed. This can be valuable to you as a leader. If your company is large enough, you probably have several people that naturally keep notes and files above and beyond the basic requirements of conducting business.

THE CHEERLEADER ENCOURAGER

SOME PEOPLE ARE the cheerleaders of the group. They encourage and help to bring about agreement in a group. Their purpose is to create cooperation and work towards the common goal.

At times, you may experience employees or associates who appear to be more interested in competing with each other than participating in teamwork. They actually may have the organization's best interests at heart, but their actions don't always reflect that. The "Cheerleader" of your group is best able to minimize intra-group competition that detracts from unity.

THE PEACE MAKER

THIS PERSON IS the one who is the natural intermediary between others. They can see things from all angles and will be of great assistance in handling difficult people and issues. Interpersonal skills are a peacemaker's forte, and he or she can be relied upon to minimize conflict, whether it is professional or personal in nature.

THE DISRUPTOR

FOR THOSE MEMBERS of your team who create problems, it is best to confront them about the issues personally and then work out the differences. Confrontation is difficult for many people. They tend to think it is only negative. However, if it is handled as information and not personal judgment, it can be constructive and may help build relationships that make your organization stronger.

We tend to think that others see the world the same way we do. If we have a great idea, everyone else should agree. However, you and I know that's not how business works. Does the culture or how you do things in your organization reflect an open-door policy that is accepting of input from employees at all levels? Are people recognized publicly for ideas that are instituted into office policy or procedures?

I met a woman who worked as an HR director in a mid-sized company who thought that employees exercised an open-door policy across all levels of the organization. However, the reality was that most employees felt inhibited by the structure of authority and were forced to keep their thoughts and feelings to themselves. If they went to a direct supervisor, the response was "Do what you were told." Retaliation was then inflicted later if the employee went above the supervisor to their manager. Ill feelings and unprofessional behavior were built up throughout the departments.

"Teambuilding" has almost become trite as a term, but we are going to take a look at it together in the context of how it applies to your organization. First, consider essential skills that are needed for it to work well. This list is used during the observation portion of a seminar to show how well a team is working together. It will reveal challenges, as well.

LISTENING

HOW WE LISTEN to each other's ideas is an indication of who we are. Have you ever said to someone, "Are you listening? Did you hear me?" Some people don't realize that they are different. How often do you find your own thoughts wandering to something else instead of actively paying attention to the person speaking? When people in your organization get together, do they build on each other's ideas? Do they consider what each other is saying and then see what else they can brainstorm together?

QUESTIONING

THIS ASPECT OF teamwork involves how we question each other. Does everyone participate in both questions and answers? As a consultant I watch how the members of the team talk together and how they respond to each other's questions. I can see if their interaction is cooperative or creates a stressful situation. When a team communicates and gets along well with each other they can discuss concerns and thoughts with each other and reach a consensus on what a solution is for a problem. People don't act threatened when questioned by other members of the team if they practice mutual acceptance. Part of the process in developing a cohesive organization is to reach a point where questions are only part of the conversation and used as a tool to get others to see a different point of view or consider something new. What types of attitudes do we see between people?

PERSUASION

IN THIS AREA, people are exchanging, defending, and rethinking ideas. For some of us, this friendly banter quickly breaks down into an argument, but it need not regress. If you were ever a member of a debate team, you learned the difference between making valid points that support or defend your point of view and stating unsupported opinions. Persuasion is actually an art that requires skill development and training, and this should be offered to employees on all levels.

RESPECT

WE SHOULD ALWAYS respect the opinions of others, regardless of whether we agree with them or not. Sometimes we have to just agree to disagree. Encouraging and supporting the ideas and efforts of others is a sign of teamwork that is essential to success. This involves how we communicate, work together, and coordinate between areas of the organization. It involves individuals as well as your mission.

HELPFULNESS

THIS IS WHERE leadership gets practical and affects our daily abilities to accomplish what needs to be done. We cannot function in this world alone. As the poet John Donne wrote, "No man is an island." We are created to rely on each other. Indeed, relying on other members of a group is not a weakness; it's a strength. I've learned that one of the best ways to help each other is to assist someone else in reaching their goals and vice versa. Helpfulness is what happens when lifting a load is too much for one person. Two people can lift together, and what was a problem for one is now an easy task for two.

To go a step further with this, I think this virtue also applies to networking. As an active member of several networking groups and a consultant for Bob Proctor, I can tell you that helping each other through these networks makes a huge difference in reaching goals. No one who makes a difference in the world is an island. In our ever-shrinking world, it's important to interact with others.

The great thing about encouraging the virtue of helpfulness is that it always comes back to benefit you, ten-fold. For instance, I found it interesting that most people can count close friends and casual acquaintances to a number of one-hundred. If we share a skill or concept with each one of them, and then they share with each of their contacts, the number of people involved in the process is 10,000. Each one of those people share with another one-hundred, and you've reached 1,000,000. From there the network quickly builds to one hundred million and continues to multiply. These original one-hundred contacts have now built a network of millions! Consider the possibilities!

I suppose Bill Gates and others are a part of the technology that enables us to create this global network. Networking allows us to exchange information and increases our ability to generate income.

SHARING

THE VIRTUE OF sharing relates closely with helping others. However, it is the opportunity for people in the organization to offer ideas and report their findings to each other. Instead of each person doing all their own research or reinventing the wheel each time a project comes up, people share what they have with others to make things work more smoothly and efficiently.

PARTICIPATION

ACHIEVING GOALS AND getting the desired results cannot happen if no one participates. Each person must do their part. It is like constructing a puzzle. If you don't have all the pieces in the right place, then the picture is not what it is supposed to look like. This also includes a step from sharing and helping. When your part is finished, you can help others complete their part of the task. This is best accomplished by incorporating all of the previous characteristics into your business culture. When individual members have clear expectations communicated to them, and are treated as valuable members of the organization, these members will be most likely to participate regularly and enthusiastically.

Without all seven of these characteristics, your organization or network will not run smoothly. You will find yourself bogged down with the obstacles. It's partly a mindset, but it's also the actions that reflect the organization and you as the manager or CEO.

Now that we have briefly examined some of the structural aspects of organizations and groups, let's go beyond that. The behavior in your organization does not always reflect the dictates of the personnel manual. In other words, people don't always do what the structural rules say to do in particular situations. Too often people apply a structural fix for a personal or relationship problem. Guess what? It doesn't work. You may think that you've solved the problems by writing a new personnel manual and reorganizing your flow chart, but what's on paper isn't what you are watching on a daily basis.

"Listen, everybody! There's no limit to how high we can fly!
We can dive for fish and never have to live on garbage again!"
--from Jonathan Livingstone Seagull

ORGANIZATIONAL BEHAVIOR IS defined as the study of organizations by examining several aspects, including economics and sociology. These concepts are related to the disciplines of behavioral psychology, strategic management, human resources and industrial psychology. We aren't going to delve too deeply into all of those here, but it is important to realize that they are integrated into the way your organization performs.

We've already looked at the individual elements that make up group dynamics. This supplies us with just another piece to the puzzle. I'd like to take a little time to look at some of the theories that apply to organizations in general. When we go into the next circle past group dynamics, we get into what some who study organizational behavior call the "macro" organizational theory. The macro level considers the whole organization and how they adapt to circumstances, as well as the structures and strategies guiding them. There are others who envision an additional circle called the "meso" organizational theory. The meso level is focused on power, culture, and networks of individuals who are a part of the overall organization. The meso level looks at the strategies and structures that guide the organization. Whenever people interact in organizations, many factors come into play. Organizational studies attempt to understand and model these factors. Like other social sciences, organizational studies seek to explain the "how" and the "why" related to your results.

I want to touch a few of these theories. You may have studied them before, but I want to discuss basics and show how they work with the concepts in this book. Each theory is actually a goal-oriented process, and goals are important to my message.

BUREAUCRACY MODEL

THIS IS ACTUALLY a sociological concept that is applied to organizations. This model supplies an explanation for the way an administrative structure sets into motion and enforces rules or laws over an organization. Bureaucracy tends to be aggressive but consistent. This model is linear and has a definite hierarchy and line of authority. While it is formal, there may be informal networks within it that connect people. Bureaucractic business models are also criticized by many people for setting up a privileged few and ignoring the needs of those lower on the ladder. Some examples of these types of organizations are governments, the armed forces, corporations, hospitals, and schools.

RATIONAL DECISION-MAKING MODEL

IN THIS MODEL, the process is logical and follows an orderly path from identifying a problem through finding the solution. The Rational Decision-Making Model has seven steps. The first step is often overlooked. If the problem is not identified in the same way by everyone, it can multiply. Each person thinks they know the problem, but instead, his or her understanding of the problem is influenced by their own viewpoint, experiences, and biases. It's important that everyone in the organization understands the problem. Then, everyone is working toward the same solution.

The second step is like brainstorming. You generate all the solutions that you can. It is best done in groups and taps into everyone's perspective. After alternative solutions are written down, then you have to do research to support each one so that the best decision can be made based on the information.

Third, the information gathered has to be evaluated and measured for the success or failure of the decision. The fourth step is to base your decision-making on the assessment process of step three. You choose the best solution. These four steps create the core for this model. The last three steps are to implement your decision into action, evaluate a chosen alternative, and modify your decision or actions if needed.

This model requires that your information is the best and most accurate to support your decision. It does have its limitations. The rational-decision making model is based on the assumption that there is only one best solution to a problem, and takes a lot of time and information. It also makes assumptions that we live in a rational and reasonable world that is apolitical. The model has a tendency to put the organization in the position to compromise for something that is "good enough." I don't know about you, but the last thing I want to do personally or professionally is to settle for something less than what I should be able to enjoy.

RESOURCE DEPENDENCE THEORY

TO ME, THIS is one of the worst business models, and you see it in too many businesses. It comes from a viewpoint of lack. You're boxed in by a way of thinking that keeps you looking at your limitations and not your possibilities. This model is governed in many ways by outside forces, for example, the price of gasoline, the availability of materials, or the number of skilled people that are in your area. This way of thinking focuses on what you don't have.

There are several other models, but I don't want to waste your time on things that demonstrate the limitations your organization can experience. I wanted to look at these as a comparison to the success and wealth that can be obtained through the concepts of this book. I'm not saying that everything about each of these models is going to spell disaster for you, but many aspects will keep you at the same level you are now. They don't allow you and those around you to explore new territory and abundance.

Business men and women who are trained in models like these are subject to what much of the world is limited by. Why let yourself stay there? Why not take what things can be applied from them and combine them with proven successful philosophies like those discussed in my seminars?

One of the main things I'm trying to point out is that the answer to your problems or challenges in business is that change cannot be structural only. I've learned that the answer must be focused on finding and using a different mindset and skill set.

Before we move on to discuss communications in your organization, I want to touch on a few more challenges you may be experiencing in your company. Many businesses have functional departments that interact in some aspects, but not in others. In some cases, each area may be somewhat isolated from other departments. What happens when there is a crisis or a short-term demand for more resources in one area? Do people from other areas step up and take on extra duties to help? Do they ignore the situation and use the excuse, "It isn't my job"? Are they oblivious to the needs of others?

Lack of cross-functional support can be devastating to your bottom line. This pitfall has been known to sink companies at times, given the right circumstances. I'm sure you don't want that for yourself or your business. Too many times we forget that in business as well as in our personal lives, we are here to share and to give to each other. We need each other to be all that we can be.

I love a quote by Deepak Chopra and think that it is relevant to this discussion of supporting one another and giving to each other. Chopra was born in 1946 in India, and is a medical doctor and a writer. He has studied philosophy and spirituality extensively.

Practicing the Law of Giving is very simple: if you want joy, give joy to others; if you want love, learn to give love; if you want attention and appreciation, learn to give attention and appreciation; if you want material affluence, help others to become materially affluent. In fact, the easiest way to get what you want is to help others get what they want. This principle works equally well for individuals, corporations, societies, and nations. If you want to be blessed with all the good things in life, learn to silently bless everyone with all of the good things in life.
-- Deepak Chopra

SOME OF THE other challenges you may be facing are high turnover rates, loss of productivity, or friction. Once again, as you know, these are related to your bottom line financially and your feeling of success.

Imagine if you could change all the things we've mentioned in your organization. Maybe you only have one or two of these concerns, or maybe you have something that I haven't mentioned in this chapter. What I want you to do is think about what it would be like to scratch the itch that you can't reach.

I can help you change your organization and your personal life for the better. Together, we can work towards reducing friction in your life. Wouldn't it be great to keep stress to a minimum in all aspects of your daily activities? You can start the ball rolling and begin creating a more spontaneous and supportive organization that encourages the input of all members, not just a few isolated people. You can change the whole culture of your organization.

Conversations will turn from gossip and unproductive talk to an atmosphere of support. You will focus on the results you truly want. As a group, you will be drawn together to work toward the common goal, not split up into individual factions that only slow down your success.

These kinds of changes work best if people are led into them. Change is not something that you force on someone else. I found that my acceptance and openness to a different way of thinking was a drastic and positive experience. If you look around you, you will find that there are not that many people you come into contact with who can lead you into the most abundant life you can imagine. Change can't be managed. Change needs to be embraced.

LEADERSHIP EXERCISE

We will continue to consider issues that affect your organization and how it runs. Spend some time considering these.

What influence or mark do you currently see that you have made on your organization? What is your imprint?

_____

_____

_____

_____

_____

_____

What imprint would you like to see? It's okay to dream big with this one. Don't limit yourself.

_____

_____

_____

_____

_____

_____

_____

Do you have an open-door policy? How does it work?

_____

_____

_____

_____

_____

_____

What is your formal organizational structure?

_____

_____

_____

_____

_____

_____

_____

What is your informal organizational structure? It may be different from the one described in the chapter.

_____

_____

_____

_____

_____

_____

POINTS TO REMEMBER

You, more than anyone else, imprint your organization.

Groups include an informal structure of personalities that can help you succeed in reaching your goals when you know how to work with them. They include the following:

- Formal Leader
- Informal Leader
- Devil's Advocate
- Note Taker
- Cheerleader Encourager
- Peace Maker
- Disruptor

- Team building requires several basic skills:
- Listening
- Questioning
- Persuasion
- Respect
- Helpfulness
- Sharing
- Participation

The organizational models commonly used are not always the best way for a business to operate. Be open to other concepts that can improve your success.

Practice a giving spirit in all things.

Embrace change.

Chapter Four

COMMUNICATION

Chapter Four

COMMUNICATION

"Everything in the world we want to do or get done,
we must do with and through people."
-- Earl Nightingale

WE TOUCHED ON communication in addressing the organization and how it is affected by people within that culture. Here I want to be more specific about the difference between communication blocks and open communication. During my years as a professional coach to business people, one of the processes we go through together is one of discovery. Even though they have several years or more in business, some leaders are still doing what they do because that's what they do. If we get stuck in old practices, policies or ways of thinking, we can't reach goals that don't fit our mold.

Step out of the mold you are in and become more. Let's look at the different ways in which people communicate. Communication begins with how we listen to each other. Do we make eye contact? Do we actually hear what the other person is saying, or do we just listen to a few words and assume we know what they are going to say? I hate to say it, but none of us are mind readers. There is a catchy saying that quips, "Most of us get our exercise jumping to conclusions, not actually going to the gym." Perhaps this is not far from the truth.

What this says about us is that we are too busy with our own concerns to pay attention to someone else. We may miss a jewel that will be buried and never surface again. This lack of communication between two people becomes an obstacle to the future exchanges of ideas. The employee feels that what they have to say has no value, or they may become bitter over being ignored. They will learn to keep their thoughts to themselves, or worse yet, talk to a third party about their experience. The ignored employee feels resentment. This resentment also builds in the third person, who is now involved and in the middle. They don't want to be in the middle of two people who can't clearly communicate with each other, and the last thing they want to do is relay messages.

Many times it is unintentional, but we get lost in our own thoughts and fade out of a conversation, only getting part of the message. Someone once said that missing a word or getting the wrong word "is like the difference between a lightening bug and lightening." The consequences can be devastating.

Patterns of communication develop with the culture of an organization and influence how results are reached. They can create an open road or one filled with pot holes. Let's take a few minutes to look at the different types of communication that are found in every organization. They include the following:

Communicating up and down your personnel chart/structure
Formal or informal communication
Verbal communication
Body language
Written memos
Email messages

WHEN WE TALK about communications up and down your personnel structure, this is one of the more formal lines of information exchange. In some organizations, this is a rule that is strictly followed. No one talks to anyone who is above their own supervisor. News travels up the ladder one position at a time. Sometimes the message can be clouded by the time it gets to your office at the top. If someone is known for a "shoot the messenger" reception of bad news, people may soften the message in order not to be blamed for delivering a negative message.

Informal lines of communication can be brief moments by the water cooler or over lunch between employees. I've found, as I'm sure you have, that sometimes the "grapevine" works better than any of our formal avenues of sharing information. This can become a destructive thing if it's centered on gossip and rumors.

Communication can be formal between people who perceive themselves as different levels of authority or informally around the water cooler. Intrapersonal communication is what goes on inside you. Interpersonal communication is between two or more people. Then we have group communications. Each one has its effect on your results.

What we term as "good" communications will make your information and productivity flow smoothly. "Bad" communications tend to put up road blocks and hinder your success rate. Yet, "good" and "bad" are only words that indicate what we perceive reality to be, using our subjective judgment. My seminars get us past that type of judgment and explore the actual interchange of information.

Sometimes we interpret what others are saying by overlaying our own thoughts and feelings instead of actually listening to what that person is saying. Part of communication is actively listening to the other person. Start by engaging in eye contact. Don't let your mind wander to the pile of papers on your desk or where you're going on vacation in two days. I know this is pretty elementary, but we tend to forget the obvious.

For example, if you are walking through the halls of your offices and one of your employees stops you to let you know about a situation, do you jump to conclusions? You may think you already know what they are going to say. The problem with that is that most of us are not very good mind readers.

If the man or woman has their arms folded as you talk with them, what does that mean? Traditionally, crossed arms indicate that the person is feeling protective of themselves or defensive. Is this always correct? Maybe not. For some people, crossed arms give them something to do with their hands. Many times if it is a woman, the only reason her arms are crossed is because she is feeling cold.

I'm not saying that body language doesn't send an unspoken message; I am saying that you need to be careful interpreting what you think it means. Body language can indicate whether someone is shut down, offended, happy, open, or skeptical. Use physical clues as part of the message, not the entire message.

I want to share with you one more thing about body language, and then I will leave the rest to be covered in our seminar. If your relationships with others are not going well, you need to look at your own behavior. The way you interact is a reflection of your attitudes and feelings toward yourself. For example, if you feel internal anger or resentment, those around you will hear it in your words or see it in your body language. If you are not aware of the message you're sending, it may surprise you when you receive an angry or resentful response from others. If you approach a situation with a positive mindset or open mind, you'll more likely receive a positive reaction.

One of the biggest problems that you can experience in your organization is when people don't confront the person with whom they have a difference of opinion. Instead, they talk to someone else about what they don't want or don't like. This doesn't help you get the situation resolved; third-party communication builds barriers and hard feelings where there may not have been before.

I've learned over the years that one of the things we need to do is discover how others communicate and what they think. Don't make a snap decision about what you think they mean. A tool that I'm familiar with and have used over the years in working with is psychometric testing. Psychometric testing helps me find out where to begin. Most people who read this book are probably knowledgeable about this type of testing and people mapping. For those of you who are not, we will briefly discuss them and touch on how I use them as a consultant.

Psychometric tests are divided into two types. One is a personality questionnaire. This type helps you learn the "why" of each employee or yourself. It is a great indicator of how people will act in different circumstances. They are not timed tests, so the person can relax and answer the questions without the pressure of a ticking clock. Another aspect that assists the person taking the test is that there is no right or wrong answer. Whatever their answer is helps me find out the best way to approach them. I believe this test gives us a way to get to know someone else in a non-threatening way. Another advantage to this type of testing is that you can take it yourself and it acts as a self-assessment. The personality test helps us better understand our preferences and how they relate to our strengths and challenges. It gives more direction to me in understanding your abilities and how they relate to your professional and career choices.

The personality questionnaire usually has eighteen or so questions that you answer about yourself. It gives you a choice of two descriptions or words to choose from. "Caring and warm" or "pushy and always right" are the choices given in an example on ActualMe.com. After the test is completed, it is analyzed and provides a picture of what style of communicator you are.

There are four styles: left-brain abstract, right-brain abstract, left-brain concrete, and right-brain concrete.

LEFT-BRAIN ABSTRACT

A **LEFT-BRAIN** abstract person emphasizes facts and information. They are systematic and detail-oriented. They like to carefully analyze all the facts before they make a decision. They abide by the rules. People with this style are disciplined, logical, and predictable.

RIGHT-BRAIN ABSTRACT

THE RIGHT-BRAIN abstract person is usually visionary and can see what the big picture is. It is important for them to know how things relate to each other. They are creative and like to consider all of their options before they make a decision. In addition, they absorb information and then process it before using it. They are not as concerned about the small details.

LEFT-BRAIN CONCRETE

A PERSON WITH a left-brain concrete style loves action and enjoys a challenge. It is what makes them tick. They are goal-oriented and want immediate accomplishments. This person always meets their deadline and works well under the pressure it brings. They don't usually want to be concerned with details. It is most important for them to take short steps to success, not a long drawn-out process. A decisive person, they want to get things done quickly. They are results-driven even more than other styles.

RIGHT-BRAIN CONCRETE

THE RIGHT-BRAIN concrete is a people person. They are caring and supportive. Warm and inviting, they interact well with everyone. They are good listeners, intuitive, and react well during change. They can adapt to changing situations. This style can be very persuasive with others.

When I work through finding out what style my clients are, we use this information as a basis and move on to using this information about ourselves to make us into more efficient communicators. Please note here that all of us tend to flex among the styles depending on what our role is. However, we do have a style that we feel most comfortable in and that is where we spend most of our time.

The second part of the psychometric tests is an aptitude test. This isn't an intelligence exam and it doesn't test for general knowledge. What it does do is look at the person's numerical, verbal and abstract reasoning abilities. The format for this part of the testing is usually multiple choices. Different from the personality testing, this test does have right and wrong answers. An aptitude test is timed and you are encouraged to move quickly from one question to another in order to complete as many as possible. The results from the aptitude test can help you understand your abilities and how they relate to your career choices.

A sample taken from Psychometric Advantage consists of twenty-seven questions to be answered in thirty minutes. A question that would be found in the Numerical section of the test could be like the following example:

Question: What is the missing number?
1 4 9 ? 25
Answer: 16

Another sample question they provided was in reference to a graph shown on the test.

Question: Which company's sales were most consistent throughout the year?
This question was the first of several about the same graph.

THIS SYSTEM OF testing is a good tool for directing me in how I can assist you most efficiently. Sometimes aptitude tests enable us to find some clues to communication problems that we might not have uncovered otherwise. I have found success in working with others by using this information and then moving on to combine it with Bob Proctor's concepts and laws for success.

This explanation of psychometric testing is generic. However, I use the Insights Psychometric Testing as a consultant and find it an integral part of the process as I guide my clients along the way.

One of the best things about beginning with the realization of who we are is that it gives us a firm foundation to build on. Your attitude is reflected by your actions. It is part of you that you bring into this discovery process.

"A great attitude does much more than turn on the lights in our worlds;
it seems to magically connect us to all sorts of
serendipitous opportunities that were somehow absent before the change."
--Earl Nightingale

During a seminar we work together to discover who you are and then validate your feelings. Some people have never had anyone validate their feelings. Too many times in life, we are told that what we feel can't be right. It's a painful, damaging experience that goes back as far as childhood. Below you may recognize some common feelings and the invalidating responses in return.

I'm cold.- No, you're not. It's warm in here.
I'm hungry. – You can't be. We just ate.
I'm thirsty. – No you're not. You can wait for a drink.
I have to go to the bathroom. – You can wait.
My leg hurts. – No, it doesn't.
My feelings are hurt.- Toughen up. Get over it.
I would be good at this job. – You don't have the qualifications.
I am an expert. – You don't have the credentials.

WE HAVE ALL experienced these and other statements or beliefs about ourselves that have been invalidated by parents, teachers, or employers. I want you to say to yourself, "Just because someone else disagrees with what I think, say, or feel doesn't mean it isn't true." We live in a world where we seldom experience validation. I work hard to change that in my seminars.

Understanding ourselves better and knowing how to communicate with others' styles makes a huge difference in your success and realizing the results you want. Improved communication skills are one of the steps we can take together.

Let's look at people mapping briefly. It helps us understand how the environment and other people influence our behavior change. Behavior is said to have reasons but not causes, and understanding the reasons, like knowing the "why," improves our communication. It examines the unconscious and how it influences our habits. These are the things we do automatically without thinking first. I'm sure you are aware that not all behaviors are appropriate in every circumstance. This type of profiling helps positively reinforce the fact that people can change. They can be versatile, and it's not a negative experience.

"To effectively communicate, we must realize that we are all different in the way we perceive the world and use this understanding as a guide to our communication with others."
--Anthony Robbins

ACCORDING TO ALBERT Mehrabian, Professor Emeritus of Psychology at UCLA, there is a definite relationship in interpersonal communications that combines words, tone of voice, and body language. Below is a breakdown of the way messages are actually communicate when someone speaks:

7% through word content

38% through tone of voice – interpretation

55% through context, body language – interpretation

In other words, communication is 7% about what you say and 93% about who you say it to!

Most of what we have been discussing in this chapter about communication is called intercommunication. That is what takes place between two or more people. It is outside of us. I'd like to take a little time to look at intra-communication with you. This is what takes place inside your mind all the time.

Intra-communication can be a more powerful force than those things around you. What you say to yourself and hear on "tapes" that play over and over in your brain may have come from other people originally, but they are no longer from the outside. Sometimes these tapes even wake you up in the middle of the night or distract you when you're driving. A thought triggers an old response, and you find yourself having a conversation in your head that took place before.

You still hear the things that were said to you. We've looked at some of those examples earlier. That is intracommunication at its worst. However, if you are playing tapes of encouragement and good thoughts for your future in your mind, you will notice the work of a powerful, positive influence.

Too often, we think that intercommunication is what transpires between our organization and another organization. We think that intra-communication is within our own organization. That is true, but I want you to consider it as your own thought process and beliefs for the purpose of this book. We will discuss image in a later chapter, but keep this in the back of your mind.

As we have discussed in this chapter, many people don't know how to communicate with others. My experience in the corporate world shows me that professional and personal relationships suffer when we don't understand ourselves or others. Corporations spend millions every year on productivity polls conducted by outside companies. Each employee is interviewed or completes a survey, and the results are tabulated and interpreted in an expensive report. The problem is that statistics show that money thrown at productivity only increases the results by fifteen percent, at the most. Wouldn't you like to do better than the corporate average?

Let's go back to your thought process as communication. Consider what would happen if you started each day with the thought, "Today I am wealthier and happier than I was yesterday." Stay with me; this not just another positive reinforcement for its own sake. It is part of a process that takes place inside of you that will affect your business and your success.

You are the one in charge of your thoughts and your results. Put those thoughts to work for you. Bob Proctor puts it this way, "You are merely using your divine nature to choose your thoughts which will build an idea. In our case, the idea happens to be that of Great Personal Wealth or True Financial Success." Isn't that what you wanted when you got into business?

You can create the future you want. It can start with this book and with the follow-up seminars. I can be contacted at susan.bagyura@ lifesuccessconsultants.com. This process made me more successful than I had ever believed I could be, and it can make a difference for you.

Focus on the thoughts that will bring you closer to your goals. Associate with people who are part of that path, and build a network that will encourage you and help you along the way. It begins with internal communication as well as good communication skills within your organization.

I used to think from a different starting point, much like you probably do. I thought about what I could accomplish with what I had instead of stretching outside my box and looking at all the possibilities. What an amazing transformation I went through when I changed my outlook and my inner voice!

We can literally self-destruct if we don't change how we think. Have you ever watched a baseball team that hasn't won very many games in years? Each spring they come out to training and go through the motions. They practice for hours in hopes of having a better season than last year. Maybe they lost their best player to another team as a free agent. Do they concentrate on the talent they still have on the team? No. They focus on what they don't have anymore.

For the first several games of the season, the team plays fairly well. They win a few, but lose more than they win. The new pitcher decides that he is tired of losing and starts talking to the other players in the dressing room, over dinner after an out-of-town game, and on the plane. He sees a vision of the team placing in the season finals. At first, others laugh. However, the pitcher keeps talking about it and encouraging his teammates at practice.

During the next hometown game, one of the mediocre players hits a home run with two players on base. They win the game. Now there are two people on the team who believe they can turn their record around. The coach trades a couple of players with another team, and the outfielders stop dropping the ball. More fans start coming to the next series at home.

Over the season, the pitcher continues to believe in himself and the team. The other players, one by one, have thoughts of winning. By the end of the season, the team had experienced a comeback season. They didn't win the pennant, but they came close. The following season they played in the first World Series in years. It all began with one person thinking one thought, "We can be a winning team."

The intra-communication spread to intercommunication with the other players and set a fire that couldn't be put out. That same process can make a difference in your success.

I want to share this lesson once more before we move on. I've learned through my time in the corporate world over the past twenty years that companies have invested billions of dollars, euros, pounds, whatever currency, on technology with the desired result of increasing the productivity of their employees. However, the overall increase in productivity has only been about fifteen percent. What companies have actually found is the real barrier to increasing productivity has been communication problems with the organizations. When communication problems are left to fester in an organization, serious situations can develop, as we've discussed in this chapter. In some organizations, communication breakdown causes an "us" against "them" situation, and the whole concept of teamwork becomes an internal battle.

We need to understand our communications style, but also that of our colleagues, counterparts and clients.

LEADERSHIP EXERCISE

We've looked at the influence of communications, people's different styles, and explored methods of learning how to communicate with each other better. These questions are meant to get you thinking about what you want to change in your own organization. You're not looking for the solutions, just a snapshot of what your culture looks like. I can help you in working through the identification of problems and solutions.

Is it a challenge for you to communicate with some people? Explain or give at least one example that comes to mind.

_____

_____

_____

_____

_____

_____

_____

What types of communication do you see in your organization?

_____

_____

_____

_____

_____

_____

Which types are positive and show positive results? _____

_____

_____

_____

Which types are negative and need to be changed? _____

_____

_____

_____

_____

How do you and those in your organization handle confrontation?
(There may be better ways that I can teach you and your organization.)

_____

_____

_____

_____

_____

_____

_____

POINTS TO REMEMBER

WE COMMUNICATE IN everything we do and say.

- Miscommunication and lack of communication are root causes for most of your problems.
- Just because the framework for communication is established doesn't mean that it works well.
- Your positive or negative mindset affects communications within your organization.
- Confrontation is not a "bad word."
- Psychometric testing can be a tool in understanding yourself, your employees, and associates better.
- Intercommunication is between departments, people, or organizations.
- Intra-communication focuses on your internal thoughts.

Chapter Five

MISSION AND IMAGE

Chapter Five

MISSION AND IMAGE

"It's the little things you do that can make a big difference. What are you attempting to accomplish? What little thing can you do today that will make you more effective? You are probably only one step away from greatness."
--**Bob Proctor**

FEW CORPORATIONS OR organizations conduct business without a mission statement. Employees see it printed on the front page of their personnel manual on their first day of work. They walk past framed copies in the hallways. The mission statement is everywhere, but how many employees could state the mission or objective of your business. Some may paraphrase it, especially if it is one that was developed by a committee and is a full page of ten-point lettering. In my experience, I've learned that most employees have, at best, only a vague idea of their company's mission statement.

Your mission and your image are inseparable. Where you go professionally is grounded in what you see yourself accomplishing. If you see your corporation reaching a particular benchmark, do you also see what you want it to look like one year, two years, or five years past that point? Know who you are corporately and individually, and it will form a stepping stone for even more success. If you are a small company, getting your image and direction fully coordinated can open up a completely new universe to you full of promise and reward.

One and Only You
Every single blade of grass,
And every flake of snow—
Is just a wee bit different . . .
There's no two alike, you know.

From something small, like grains of sand,
To each gigantic star
All were made with THIS in mind:
To be just what they are!

How foolish then, to imitate—
How useless to pretend!
Since each of us comes from a MIND
Whose ideas never end.

There'll only be just ONE of ME
To show what I can do—
And you should likewise feel very proud,
There's only ONE of YOU.
That is where it all starts
With you, a wonderful
unlimited human being.
--James T. Moore

SINCE YOUR IMAGE and mission are linked so closely, we need to examine your self-image first. Reexamining your belief system is difficult and unsettling. That's because our belief system represents how we perceive ourselves. Self-examination takes a lot of courage. This type of introspection can make you feel unsure of who you are and what your place is in life. The experience can give you the sensation of feeling out of control. That is exactly what keeps many people from ever questioning their own values, assumptions and beliefs.

In most cases, these are things we've embraced since childhood. But what if some of them aren't true? What if reality is not the image I've tried to maintain?

STEP ONE

THE FIRST STEP is to define your preferred beliefs. Make some choices. Some beliefs you may want to hold onto, but others you will want to release. The most important part of this process is for you to be honest with yourself. You need to be willing to become the person you really want to be and change those things about yourself that keep you from being all that you can be. You may be the largest obstacle in your path that prevents you from realizing the financial success you are capable of obtaining.

Don't allow yourself to slip into a state of denial. You are only deceiving yourself and standing in your own way. I've learned that I have to get out of my way to progress. When we are able to define who we are and what we really want out of life, we can experience a clarity that we haven't had before. This clarity may help you find your true purpose in life, both personally and professionally.

I encourage you to step out on faith and leave behind the old you. Stop looking for an easy way out. The easy way out can be deceiving and lead you down a path that keeps you from true success. It is better to deal with issues that affect you and the world around you. It may be past circumstances, past relationships, or significant events found in your past. It is time to keep the lesson and move on. Don't let the "old you" ruin the future for the "real you."

STEP TWO

HONESTY WITH YOURSELF doesn't mean you need to confront all of your issues at once. However, it does mean you need to take an impartial look at your issues. Then you need to accept them unconditionally. I've learned that identifying my own issues allows me to get in touch with my authentic self. After you take that first step, it is much easier to find your life's purpose and sets you up to pursue your passion.

Practicing honesty in every part of your life would actually make life simpler. It's often difficult to do at first because we're so used to using our old programmed belief system as a crutch. Dishonesty complicates your life and traps you in a web of lies and pretenses that drains your energy. How can you reach your life's purpose and get the results you want to experience if you remain in that web? Being honest releases a great amount of energy and frees you from those unnecessary distractions that get in your way.

"You don't have to rehearse to be yourself."
-- unknown

THIS IS TRUE. It's much easier and takes far less energy to remember one story. Like any habit, honesty gets easier with practice, but it does something else, too. It gives other people around you the permission to be honest, too. When you incorporate it into your personality and behavior, people recognize who you are and what you want. They give you more respect if you are real and authentic. Honesty gets rid of unrealistic expectations that people put on you. It also lets others know exactly where they stand with you. I know I prefer that type of relationship with others.

Being honest with yourself and others is the beginning of taking total responsibility for your present and your past. Challenging your own belief system is not an easy challenge to face, much less progress through. I hope you will keep reading. We're going to cover basics here to build on later.

As adults, we are completely responsible for our choices and outcomes. Too many people waste time blaming others or circumstances for what has gone badly for them. I've learned from experience that this attitude leaves me powerless in every sense except for one, self-destruction.

In most cases, the results you continue to experience can be traced back to some decision you either made or avoided making. You may disagree on the surface, but we are affected by those decisions we've been a part of either consciously or subconsciously. Once you stop denying that you are at fault, you've crossed the first bridge. Then you can quit blaming others, and you can begin accepting your part to play in every one of the circumstance and experiences of your life.

You will then be in a better position to move past your obstacles and learn from your mistakes. I know it's not easy. I went through this same process myself, and I have a much more successful life than I had before. Some people get angry to hear that they are responsible for their lot in life, but it's true. Believe me; it's worth taking the time to understand this reality. Unfortunately, if you choose to deny your mistakes or refuse to take responsibility for your results, you'll fail to learn and change. Choosing to learn from our mistakes enables us to grow and succeed.

"Don't be afraid to make mistakes. Only those who dare to fail greatly can ever achieve greatly."
-- John F. Kennedy

AFTER YOU'VE EXAMINED your level of honesty, take a look at your relationships with others. Are they going well? What part of that is a direct result of your own behavior? The way you interact with others is a direct reflection of your attitude toward yourself. For example, if you experience internal anger and resentment, these emotions will come across in your words or body language, and you will receive an angry or resentful response from those around you. If you approach a situation with a positive or open mind, you will receive a positive outcome.

STEP THREE

YOU HAVE A choice. Either take responsibility for your past and current results or don't. Failing to take responsibility has serious consequences. Are you willing to pay that high of a price? How do you know if you're actually taking a healthy responsibility for your actions and decisions? Here is a list of some things for you to consider:

> *Are you angry, hostile, or depressed?*
> *Does fear direct your actions?*
> *Do you focus on failure?*
> *Are you a "people-pleaser"?*
> *Do you have an addictive personality?*
> *Are you part of a codependent relationship?*
> *Do you feel guilty all the time?*
> *Do you have trust issues with other people?*
> *Is change difficult for you?*
> *Do you consistently have difficulty making a decision?*

IN MY EXPERIENCES with clients, we've gone through considerations like these as part of the process. It is important for you as a CEO to lead by example and take responsibility for your actions and those of your organization as a reflection of you. Then, teach it to others. This process includes a matter of changing how you think about circumstances and people Personal responsibility is just the beginning. I found it gave me a feeling of more self-control and more power over my circumstances.

I suggest that before we begin working together and conduct a seminar that you prepare yourself. Begin with some of these suggestions. Once again, we will build on these:

Be willing to accept full responsibility for your actions.

Make conscious decision rather than habitual decisions.

Surround yourself with positive people.

Remember that change is not a bad word.

Allow yourself to be open to new ideas.

Be willing to let go of your past irrational beliefs.

Be willing to take a risk to become more successful.

Share with others who are trustworthy.

Overcoming your past beliefs is freeing. You will feel less inhibited and realize that they are mostly based on other people's values or ideas. You'll be pleasantly surprised how much letting all of that past baggage will allow you to accomplish. Trust me on this. Step out and make the changes. You will be rewarded over and over for your choice to do so.

If you're like most people, you believe that what is in the past is over. We think it hasn't affected us, but this isn't true. Your past has a great impact on the way you value yourself now. Remember when you were a child and thought anything was possible? How many times did someone tell you to "grow up"? Believe it or not, that type of comment has stuck with you throughout your life. Now imagine hearing those types of negativities for years. Do you see the power of programming? No wonder you feel inadequate about what you can achieve sometimes.

Were there times when someone complimented or praised you? Remember those statements when you start reprogramming your way of thinking. Get rid of statements such as "I can't" and "It's not possible." Replace those thoughts with, "Yes, I can!" Your results will change drastically.

Be willing to accept who you have been and who you are. Also, focus on what you can be in the future.

"Then let yourself love all that you take delight in.
Accept yourself whole, accept the heritage
That shaped you and is passed on from age to age
Down to your entity. Remain mysterious;
Rather than be pure, accept yourself as numerous."
- John Ashbery "Some Words"

BOB PROCTOR TEACHES that we all have a definite purpose that will guide our ambitions, vision, and ultimately our goals. Your mission is the do the thing that you love the most. Believe it or not, you can fall in love with a cause or a vision of who you can be in the future. When you fully commit yourself to this cause, you believe in it and will do what ever it takes to get there. The greatest part of being in love with what you do is that you experience a feeling of harmony that wasn't there before.

A sense of harmony happens when you and the idea, purpose, or person that you care deeply about resonates with you. Have you ever hit it off with someone that you just met and felt like you were finally home? You feel like you've known each other forever, not just a few minutes.

Your mission is a part of who you are and whether you succeed in business or not. Both the subconscious and the conscious mind are in sync and focused on the same outcome. One of the most interesting parts of this to me is that when you love and commit yourself to making an idea into a reality, it seems to guide you rather than the other way around.

"I am grateful for the idea that has used me."
--Alfred Adler

WHEN YOU ARE locked in on your purpose or mission, it is easy to get up in the morning and get to work. You look forward to each day doing what you enjoy. Finding your mission is like opening a present. It brightens your whole life. For me, I feel more ambitious, dedicated, and I never lack for motivation. Even though it feels like Christmas morning, it isn't. It's still the same day it was a few minutes ago. Do you know what the difference is? It's you. You've found your true mission. Now, enjoy the journey and the abundance in store for your future

Once you find your mission, your next step to make it a reality is by creating and focusing on a vision. Concentrate on what you see as your success. We must hold on to our dreams as tightly as we can. Too many people will try to take them from us. Sometimes they are physically trying to steal from us, but worse than that, it can be those times you share your excitement with a friend and they put you down. These are people who steal your joy! Some will laugh at you. Others will tease you. Still others may want to discourage you and then stand by to watch you fail. I've experienced those circumstances myself, and you probably have, too. Don't let others take your mission and vision away from you. You are in control of yourself.

I love sharing my successes with others and helping them to reach their goals. It brings joy to both of our lives. Don't associate with people who are always going to try to bring you down for what you are doing or what you believe. Find other friends and associates to enjoy the journey with. That is basically what this book is about. It is an invitation to you to take a journey with me. We may only travel part of it together, but we will be on parallel paths.

Van Gogh said, "I dream my painting and then I paint my dream." He knew and loved his mission in life. As he painted from his vision, the picture on the canvas took shape. He took the steps to connect his vision to his daily goals and to his mission.

My own vision began with the foundations of working in the corporate world and in marketing. My vision grew from there as my experience and knowledge grew. Then, when I added the concepts from Bob Proctor to the mix, it was like adding a rocket booster to my career. My mission became clearer. I took the action that I needed to progress down this path and continue to do so. Each morning I'm glad to see the new day. I enjoy my personal and professional life more than ever.

This enjoyment has really enhanced my marriage. My husband moves from time to time in his business, and as a consultant, I am blessed to be able to keep increasing my network of clients and associates. No matter where I go, I continue to work at the things I love. I stay in harmony with my purpose and mission. However, I have to warn you that it isn't automatic. I didn't just plug in a few thoughts, make a plan, and then sit back and watch. I must take an active role in reaching the goals I've set for myself.

I have to stay focused and involved personally in the process. I've also learned that I need to be aware that I can get so tied up in the tiny details that I never get to the big picture. That is what stops many business people from actually succeeding. If you never take the first step outside your office door, the results you're planning for probably won't happen. Another thing that I can't emphasize enough is to enjoy the journey. Too many of us go through life stuck in the details and never even look up to see the scenery or enjoy the ride. Don't let yourself miss the ride.

Sometimes people get sidetracked and confused about their mission. They can get their vision and mission confused. The mission you've locked into and love is the rock or cornerstone for your foundation on the road to success. Keep in mind that you may run into resistance. That doesn't mean you're off the path on a detour somewhere. Resistance isn't necessarily negative. Remember that the good things you are seeking to have in your life are being attracted to you.

Your image dictates your mission. Two of my favorite quotes from Chang are, "To fly as fast as thought to anywhere that is now - you begin by knowing that you have already arrived..." and, "I am a perfect expression of freedom, here and now."

LEADERSHIP EXERCISE

By considering these questions, you can focus on your image and how it relates to your purpose or mission in your personal and professional life.

Do you have a mission statement for your company? What is it? _____

_____

_____

_____

_____

_____

Do you have a mission statement for yourself? What is it? _____

_____

_____

_____

_____

_____

What is your self-image? How do you see yourself? _____

_____

_____

_____

_____

_____

_____

*What are your preferred beliefs about yourself?*_____

_____

_____

_____

_____

_____

_____

Do your beliefs conflict with reality? If so, how?
*(You may not know the answer to this, but at least contemplate it.)*_____

_____

_____

_____

_____

_____

_____

_____

_____

*What would you like to change about your image?*_____

_____

_____

_____

_____

_____

Who and what do you want to be? _____

_____

_____

_____

_____

_____

_____

_____

_____

What keeps you from being who you want to be and the mission you are meant to have?

_____

_____

_____

_____

_____

_____

_____

_____

POINTS TO REMEMBER

- Mission and image are inseparable.
- Begin with yourself, examining your values, assumptions, beliefs.
- Be totally honest with yourself and others.
- You are 100% responsible for your choices and outcomes.
- Your self-image guides your success.
- Your results have a direct line to your self-image and mission.
- If you approach every situation with a positive and open mind, you will likely receive a positive outcome.
- Churchill said, "The only thing we have to fear is fear itself."
- Use your mission as your rock and foundation for building your success.
- An additional source for you that explains the relationship between your purpose, vision, and goals can be downloaded at www.giftsforyourmind.com. Purpose Vision Goals can be downloaded as a document or MP3 from that site.

Chapter Six

BRIDGING THE GAP

Chapter Six

BRIDGING THE GAP

"Don't let the fear of the time it will take to accomplish something stand in the way of your doing it. The time will pass anyway; we might just as well put that passing time to the best possible use."
--Earl Nightingale

WE'VE BEEN LOOKING at the way your organization operates and ways in which you would benefit from my own corporate and consulting experiences. I want to continue along the same path, but start connecting those issues with some concepts that will assist you in attaining the elusive results in some areas that we mentioned in previous chapters. I want to help you obtain everything you've ever wanted or dreamed of. If you are a small, emerging company with a few employees, I can help your business grow. If you are a mid-sized company, I can help you expand into new areas of the market place and diversify. If you are already the CEO of a large and successful corporation, I want to help you reach goals that exceed your greatest dreams.

I hope you will continue to take this walk with me. I've found it exciting and exhilarating, both professionally and personally, to take this journey. I believe that one of our biggest challenges is to get over a chasm between where we see ourselves and where we actually are.

In my coaching and consulting, I look at the big picture of your organization and what it is you want to accomplish. Then I work to find what each person is thinking, feeling, expecting, and experiencing. Lastly, we move back out to the corporate way of thinking, feeling, expecting, and experiencing. We literally will change your company from the inside out and give you the organization you dream about. You personally can become wealthy in all areas of your life with these concepts. Wealth can become your reality, and I feel confident that I can assist you in getting there.

Bridging this gap takes changing in the way you see the world. I know I've said this previously, but it continues to apply. One analogy that illustrates my point is the Golden Gate Bridge. It is known all over the world as a symbol of San Francisco, an engineering marvel, and the end results of one person's idea, vision, and mission to accomplish it. It is a physical example of what persistence and focus can do. The Golden Gate Bridge spans the entrance to the San Francisco Bay.

For many, many years before the Golden Gate Bridge was built, the only way for people to get across San Francisco Bay was by ferry. If you've ever seen pictures of the Bay during the early twentieth century, you can see the problem: the water is clogged with ferries.

In the 1920's Joseph Strauss, an engineer and bridge builder, was convinced that a bridge should be built across what was called the Golden Gate. Surprisingly enough, he met many people who were opposed to his idea. Most were a part of special interest groups or the military. However, his biggest challenge wasn't people's opinions or resistance. It was the physical conditions of the area. The bridge was an enormous engineering feat.

One of the reasons a bridge had never been built there before was the physical conditions. Most people looked for an easier place to solve the problem of getting from one side of the Bay to the other. The narrows that form the mouth to San Francisco Bay often have winds of up to 60 miles an hour. Strong ocean currents sweep through a hidden, rugged canyon below the surface.

Construction on the art deco-designed bridge began in 1933. They chose International Red for the color. The project was completed four years later in 1937. A couple of interesting things about the engineer, Joseph Strauss, is that he was revolutionary in his building safety innovations. This was one of the first projects that used hard hats and conducted daily sobriety tests on the workers.

At the same time the Golden Gate Bridge was being built, another group was constructing the Bay Bridge from Oakland to San Francisco. During the years that these two bridges were built, the Bay Bridge project lost twenty four workers, while the Golden Gate project only lost twelve. What an outstanding record! This was an era when the average loss on most construction projects was one man for every one million dollars spent.

Just as Joseph Strauss made ground-breaking history in bridge building, you can apply the principles in this book to be innovative and successful. He didn't let anything stop him from bridging the gap between being a good engineer and a magnificent one. Likewise, you can make changes that can take you from being a good business man or woman to being an example of excellence.

It once again comes back to you. The decision and change starts with you. Some of the questions that we must ask ourselves when we look across the gap are as follows:

Am I experiencing success in my life?

We've discussed this previously, but whether or not you are as successful as you want to be or could be is a question that only you can answer for yourself. Then you can move on. I had been successful in the corporate world and in my marketing career, but I wanted to excel and go beyond that. I found a way through these concepts.

What about the people that I associate with? Are they successful?

Mentally take account of those with whom you surround yourself. To what extent are they happy and successful? Once you decide to focus on what you want, you will attract people and things into your life that you need in order to get what you really want.

Are they as successful as I want to be?

While you're examining the success rate of those around you, remember that not everyone wants to take the same path. However, I'm sure there are those around you who would like to be more successful than they are right now. I may leave some friends and associates behind and make new ones, but you want to surround yourself with positive thinkers.

If I continue to go along as I have in the past, where will I be five years from now?

See yourself in five years. Just what is it that you want to accomplish most? This will take some time to define for some of you. Others know exactly where they want to be five years from today. Think about it. Meditate on it.

Am I operating at or near peak efficiency?

If you don't have time for anything new, then how can you expand and grow? There may be things that can be reprioritized. This process can give you openings to change. If you're working to your capacity now and still not achieving your goals, something is wrong. We can consider what to do about it together.

Am I really a professional, or have I been doing just enough to get by?

In the first chapter we discussed some of the definitions of professionalism and what it takes to be a professional, not just a worker in an eight-to-five job. Think about your position, your training, and your experience.

Am I devoting a part of my time each day to thinking of ways and means by which I can increase my contribution to the world?

I've found that the more I contribute to my family, community, country, and world, the better my life is and the bigger difference I can make for others.

Am I really aware that my rewards in life will always be in exact proportion to my service?

Think about people who have given of themselves and their wealth to help others. They are truly wealthy in every way. In the chapter about leadership, I cited several successful and visionary businessmen that I admire. Each one of them has been involved in philanthropy to one degree or another.

Am I following an intelligent course for improving my mind and increasing my knowledge?

I believe that we should never stop learning. It should be a lifetime occupation. However, it's not just being informed that is important; it is key to take that knowledge and apply it to our lives. That is what makes the difference between mediocrity and overwhelming abundance.

Do I have a studying and reading program?

It's surprising how many people I meet that say they never have time to read. Of the people who do read on a regular basis, many of them only read for entertainment. I'm not saying there is anything wrong with sitting down with a great book and enjoying yourself; I do it myself from time to time. What I'm talking about is including in your day some time to read and to study concepts that will assist you to have a more successful and enjoyable life. One of my goals is for this book to be one of those tools coupled with a seminar.

Or do I think I already know enough?

This can be a trap. If we have gotten an education and learned from the school-of-experience in the corporate world, we may be lulled into thinking that we know all there is to know. Believe me, there are always things else to learn and stretch us. That is how we progress and continue to grow.

I expect my company, my community and my country to improve each year, but what am I doing personally to keep pace with this improvement or to exceed it?

It is up to each of us to participate in our world and help make it a better place tomorrow than it is today. As always, the improvement begins with me and spreads out one ring at a time. If each of us practices this everyday, imagine what the world will be like in one year, five years, or ten years.

Do I have a clear direction and a well-defined purpose in life? Or am I simply marking time and going along with the crowd?

In an earlier chapter we discussed how your purpose or mission and self-image are related. Think about whether or not your direction is clear, for you and for your business. If we are here just holding a place and breathing the air, then we are not coming anywhere close to who we are meant to be. If you are marking time, it's time to get up and get moving.

Am I motivated by what I really want out of life, or am I mass-motivated?

Some of us are internally motivated by the dreams we hold and the goals we want to accomplish. Others are motivated by outside influences. What motivates you? Do you let others change your mind about what path you want to take? Their advice may not always be what you need, in spite of their good intentions. That is why we've spent so much time examining ourselves. Be sure you're not letting others detour you from where you really need to be travelling.

"No horse gets anywhere until he is harnessed. No steam or gas ever drives anything until it is confined. No Niagara is ever turned into light and power until it is channelled. And no life ever grows great until it is focused, dedicated and disciplined."
--Harry Emerson Fosdick

WHEN WE LOOK at our challenges, many people think that if you throw enough money at a problem that it will be solved. Unfortunately, this is an oversimplification. Solving a problem takes more than money. Money, after all, is only one of the tools in your tool kit. In addition, we think that if we don't have enough money, we're stuck and can't reach our goals. This also is totally incorrect because it comes from a mindset of "what I don't have." It helps if we can put money in perspective. I love what Jack Canfield says about money: "What we have to get straight in our heads is that owning the money doesn't mean ANYTHING. It's the DOING with money that develops us; it's not in the having. And when you have more, you're enabled to DO more."

Many of us have been taught that seeking money is somehow bad. Those who associate money with greed and evil can never see what good money can do. It can feed the poor and clothe the homeless. Money can build shelters for people with no roof over their heads. It can contribute to providing income for those who have limited funds. These are only a few of the most obvious things that you can do with money. When you put money in the right hands, it can help hundreds or thousands of people. Having financial freedom can allow you to help people all over the world or those within your own community.

So how do you bridge the gap between a good living and wealth? Not many people have the awareness required to manifest wealth. Being able to envision and make manifest your dreams begins with your awareness and that of others. This is one of the many reasons I chose to be a consultant. Sharing my knowledge enables us to become wealthy together; we have more and can share more.

I want to share some statistics with you that I'm borrowing from the Social Security Administration. Take any group of one-hundred people at the start of their career and follow them for forty years when they most likely retire.

- Only one will be wealthy.
- Four will be financially secure.
- Five will continue working because they have to.
- Thirty-six will be dead.
- Fifty-four will be dead broke, and dependent on meager Social Security checks, relatives, friends and even charity for a minimum standard of living.
- To sum up, that means that five percent are successful; ninety-five percent are not.
- What makes this five percent different?
- There are millionaires with college degrees and millionaires with little education.
- There are millionaires in developed countries and millionaires in poor nations.
- There are millionaires who were born rich. There are people who went from homelessness to millionaire status by mastering the Law of Attraction.
- There is no single quality that stands out among the wealthy except one.

The richest people in the world, either consciously or unconsciously, have learned, understand, and use the Law of Attraction in their daily lives. It was eye-opening to me when I found out these statistics. Multimillionaires whom I know and have met feel fulfilled in life; I feel more fulfilled. We are wealthy in many ways, and it is wonderful to know that we can become all that we imagine and more. It is also fulfilling to help others find the same path. They have come to understand that abundance doesn't have to elusive; it's part of their birthright. The really great thing is that it is not a win-lose proposition. There is enough for everyone. The more we share, the more we have. However, we must learn to harness the correct thought process to attract abundance and to help others understand concepts of getting rich. That is what I teach as a consultant.

I met a woman who had lived on a limited income as a single mother with children. Each month was a struggle. Sometimes she had to count out change from a penny jar to get a few groceries to last until the next paycheck came. She operated from a mindset of lack and of "just making do." How many times do people do that and stay in the pit they are in? She told me one time that it had been so depressing for her that she had forced herself to make it into a game each time she went to the grocery store. She tried to get the most for what she had; she tried to create some type of abundance from what she thought of as nothing.

While I admired her for being a hard worker, I felt sorrow for her that she had spent so many years in need, and not just for money. I have a better solution than her game based on limits. Bob Proctor says, "We need to make a game out of earning money. There is so much good we can do with money. Without it, we are bound and shackled and our choices become limited."

If we are going to cross that chasm, then we need to have the right tools. I want to share those secrets with you and others as they were shared with me. Why let a few people enjoy all the wealth and hide the methods they use? These methods involve using the science of getting rich. Let me guide you through the system and methods that lead to the solution and successful results.

Remember when you used to play "imagine" as a child? The sky was the limit. You could see yourself doing anything. Nothing stopped you. One of my friend's sons dreamed big. He saw himself driving a Ferrari and living in a huge house in the mountains for part of the year and near the beach for the rest of it. How many little girls dream of being a prima ballerina, or for that matter, a CEO of a large corporation? Children are not hindered by life and the influences of others telling them it can't be done. They are free from all of that. Then, as they grow up, they let that freedom go. I'm saying that you must take it back.

Let me prime the pump to get your imagination started again. Here's an explanation for those of you who aren't sure what this old-fashioned term means. My grandfather used to talk about his father pouring a little water over the pump when he started pushing it up and down to help the water come up from the bottom of the well more easily. That's what we are going to do with your imagination. I'm going to give you some things to start with, and then you can let your imagination run wild. Think BIG! If you're going to manifest something, why make it small?

Imagine making a difference in thousands of people's lives through your efforts.

Imagine writing a life-changing book.

Imagine developing products that could benefit all of humanity.

Imagine creating new jobs.

Imagine bringing wisdom and enlightenment to others.

Imagine if you did all these, the kind of legacy you would leave behind for your family and community.

What will people remember about you when you're gone?

This little exercise in playing the imagine game is to stimulate you and let you release yourself to imagine and become everything you've ever wanted to be. Let's bridge that gap that keeps you from completely fulfilling your destiny.

LEADERSHIP EXERCISE

THIS EXERCISE IS to continue the contemplation we have begun in this chapter of bridging the gap. Too many of us get caught in the current and never make it across to the other side. Be willing to take another step on your road to total success. Join hands and work together to get across.

Identify one or two gaps that you are experiencing either personally or professionally.

_____

_____

_____

_____

_____

_____

Use the bottom of this page and the next one to journal your thoughts, reactions, and feelings about the questions to think about in this chapter. This is meant as an exercise to help you deal with the gaps.

_____

_____

_____

_____

_____

Do you want to change your world for the better? What can I do to help you in your endeavor?

_____

_____

_____

_____

_____

_____

_____

_____

POINTS TO REMEMBER

RECOGNIZE THAT GAPS will stand in your path, but you can get across them.

- Remember the process starts with you.
- Your rewards are in proportion to your service to others.
- It is important to continue learning and applying new information and concepts.
- Learning should be for a lifetime.
- Reading and studying are an important part of your day.
- Statistics show only five percent of working people are successful under the system most often used in gaining wealth. You can be part of changing that.
- There is enough wealth for everyone; it's not limited.
- You can bridge the gap with the tools I can give you.

Chapter Seven

CREATIVE ADVANTAGE

Chapter Seven
CREATIVE ADVANTAGE

"The key question isn't 'What fosters creativity?' But it is why in God's name isn't everyone creative? Where was the human potential lost? How was it crippled? I think, therefore, a good question might be not why do people create, but why do people not create or innovate? We have got to abandon that sense of amazement in the face of creativity, as if it were a miracle if anybody created anything."
--Abraham Maslow

I'M SURE YOU'VE been in countless brainstorming sessions throughout your career. Think about what happens in your company. If you have a research and development department, is that the only area that still shares new ideas? Are new ideas discouraged in other areas because "We don't do things that way around here," or "That's a good idea, but it won't work," or the stock comment, "We always do it this way"? These comments and beliefs in a corporation can be deadly. If you don't continue to meet the needs of the market you serve, you won't be in business for long.

Tap into your creativity and that of those around you again. It was there when you first dreamed of being where you are today. You believed in yourself and saw yourself as a CEO. Sometimes after we achieve the level we have worked towards for our career, we fail to see beyond that point. It is actually a plateau and not the end of dreams and goals.

We live in an abundant world, surrounded by opportunities that we can choose to take advantage of or not. Some of you may think that depends on what country you live in, but I'm here to let you in on a secret. It is a plentiful world no matter where you live. How you view your world and your opportunities goes back to your self-image that we discussed in chapter five.

People have a tendency to be competitive, even with others in their own departments. They look out for their own interests instead of the corporate welfare. If they develop an idea or a concept, they usually keep it close to them. Many have experienced developing a new product or procedure, only to have their supervisor take full credit for it if it is a success.

We want to work on opening people's creativity in the workplace in a non-threatening, honest, and appreciative atmosphere. Part of the process is to realize that we are here to be of service to one another. I know most people don't think about that in internal organizational departments. They tend to think of the customer as an outsider, not the person on the other end of the phone or the desk. When an organization learns to operate with a focus on teamwork and service, it is a better place to work and live, as well as more successful with its customers.

Your organization can learn to use its creativity on all plains and use friendly competitiveness to develop better products and services than your competitors in the marketplace. Too many times competition is the antithesis of creativity. When people feel competitive with those around them, it probably comes from a position of limitation and feeling of doubt or fear. They are worried that someone else will get recognition that should have come to them. Another point is that when people have low self-esteem, they try to make themselves look better than their coworkers. When we come from that place, our thoughts and personal beliefs only bring more of the same into our lives. We get exactly what we don't want.

We need to focus on excellence. I've learned that doing the best I can in all areas creates the best results. Excellence is a matter of providing the best service possible. I believe this change in our outlook and behavior is the basis for creativity.

Competition thrives on the idea that there isn't enough of something, and that is a lie. We live in an abundant universe. There is plenty for everyone. People don't have to think about taking from their neighbor in order to have what they need. In my experience, by merely helping each other get what we want, we invoke the universe to bring what we need to us. Think about it. Can you imagine what a difference there would be in your business if the client's needs were the primary concern?

When you unleash the creativity using the principles practiced in my professional seminars, your employees should experience an increase in enthusiasm over their part of the mission and develop a new passion for excelling in their own position, as well as helping to push your organization past obstacles that stand in your way.

How do you think that we got the artificial heart? Do you think that Dr. Robert K. Jarvik knew how that was going to happen? He had no idea "how," but he had a big enough "why." When Jarvik was in college taking mechanical drawing and architecture, his father's heart disease gave him the motivation to change his career path into medicine. His father was a physician and surgeon. Robert had been tinkering and inventing since he had been in high school, but his father's illness inspired him to help develop the artificial heart.

He worked with a team of artificial organ developers at the University of Utah, using their previous work and innovations of his own. By the early 1980s he had developed an artificial heart that could be implanted in a human being. Jarvik knew what he wanted to accomplish and why it was needed. Even though it took years and he wasn't able to perfect it until he worked with the team at the University of Utah, he focused his efforts towards that end. The people and the methods he needed to help him accomplish the task came together over time.

I've learned that the "how" happens by exact and universal law. There are seven universal laws that govern the way that people think and behave. When you understand these universal laws, you can apply them in your personal and professional life. When I made that transition from learning to understanding and then applying them to myself, things began to change. It can happen for you like it did for me and others I've worked with. Your results will change with a snap of the fingers.

These aren't concepts that we are taught in schools or universities. You won't find them in most business schools or management books, but they are real and they influence the results you experience, whether you agree with them or not. I believe the natural laws of the universe are so absolutely precise that we have no difficulty today in building a spaceship that we can land on the moon and can time the landing to the precision of a fraction of a second.

We have always been able to do it, but it didn't happen until the 1960s. We just didn't know "how" we were going to do it. There is a well-known story about Dr. Warner von Braun meeting with President John F. Kennedy. He sat in the Oval Office with the President discussing the space race and concerns over Russian superiority in launching the first satellite, Sputnik.

President Kennedy asked him, "How are we going to land a man on the moon? What do we need to get him there?"

Dr. von Braun listened intently to these questions. The President continued, "We need to win the space race."

Dr. von Braun said just a few words. He said, "The will to do it."

We just need the "why," as discussed previously. If you have a big enough "why," by exact universal law you will begin to attract everything necessary for its fulfilment.

Napoleon Hill was twenty-three years old when he had an opportunity to interview the richest and most successful man in the world at the time, Andrew Carnegie. At the end of a three-day interview, Carnegie commissioned Hill to write a book that the average person could read and learn the secrets of success. Hill worked on the project and also met with Edison, Rockefeller, Wilbur Wright, and Alexander Graham Bell. He also spoke with four sitting United States Presidents.

In the book entitled Thoughts Are Things, Hill realized that what these people possessed was an ability to think. He concluded in his writing that the dominating thoughts in their minds literally began to act like magnets. Their thoughts attracted to them everything requisite for their thought or dream to become a reality. They began to attract all the forces, all the people, and all the circumstances necessary that were in harmony with the ideas that they held.

He was talking about the Law of Vibration and the Law of Attraction. We are familiar with natural laws like the Law of Gravity. Whenever we apply our understanding of a specific law to a purpose, that purpose's potential is increased. Whenever we apply our understanding of a Universal Law to a specific purpose, the purpose's potential is increased.

Let me give you an example. Imagine that I have a tank of water and an iron bar. If I set the iron bar on top of the water, what happens to it? It sinks, doesn't it? Why does it sink? It's heavier than the water, right? Now that appears to be the truth. However, if you study what happens, you learn that the natural laws that govern why the iron sinks can also be applied in principle to your behavior.

Now, imagine I take a piece of balsa wood, and I set it on top of the water. What happens? The balsa wood floats, right? Why? Because it is lighter than the water. However, think about this. Not everything is as it appears to us. How do we explain cruise ships? Aircraft carriers? How do we explain super-tankers? They are all made of materials that are much heavier and denser than water, yet they float.

We link our thoughts and understanding to the law of buoyancy to a specific purpose, launching a ship, and that purpose's potential rises to the top. It expands; it increases in its potential. I've learned that when we begin to understand and apply these laws to the way we think and behave, we also rise. I hope you will stay with me. These may be new concepts and viewpoints to you, but from my own professional experiences, I know that they work. They are made clear in my seminars, as is how to apply them.

I believe that the results a person gets in his or her life are an expression of their level of awareness. Awareness is the first step to understanding. Understanding is a step on the way to application. Without application, simple awareness is like getting the booby prize instead of the sweepstakes prize. We know that in school or training, we learn to understand the essentials of the field that we are in or the business that we are in. We learn to understand the economy in which we operate. On a personal basis, we become involved in relationships with others who are important to us. We develop a spiritual connection to our creator. What then?

We have been conditioned to think that a person's results are an expression of their potential, not their thought process and focus. I would like you to recondition your thinking. The seven universal laws are a part of nature. They have been a part of the universe since the beginning. Briefly, they are the Law of Perpetual Transmutation, the Law of Relativity, the Law of Vibration, the Law of Polarity, the Law of Rhythm, the Law of Cause and Effect, and the Law of Gender. These natural laws apply to the physical planet and how the solar system works, but they also apply to how our lives are lived. We are a part of that universe.

LAW OF PERPETUAL TRANSMUTATION

THE LAW OF Perpetual Transmutation is defined as energy. Energy is. Energy is in constant change and moving into physical form and back to pure energy again. Scientists like Einstein were aware of it and studied it. Everything that we see or know is either growing or dying, increasing or decreasing.

LAW RELATIVITY

THE LAW OF Relativity says that nothing is bad or good, big or small until you relate it to something else. Everything just is until it is compared with something else. However, there are moral absolutes that we practice.

LAW OF VIBRATION AND LAW OF ATTRACTION

THE LAW OF Vibration states that everything moves. Nothing rests or remains still. Everything in the universe vibrates to a frequency. An interesting fact about this is that the denser the object, the higher the speed of vibration. At the same time, the lower the density of an object is, the lower the speed of vibration. This law also includes the Law of Attraction. Like vibrations attract others like them. It is like the old-fashioned radios. You had to locate the correct frequency to hear the music you are searching for.

LAW OF POLARITY

THE LAW OF Polarity is one that most people have heard about all their lives but haven't thought about as a law of nature. Opposites exist everywhere: hot and cold; up and down. There is a positive side and a negative side to everything.

LAW OF RHYTHM

THE LAW OF Rhythm operates everything. The tide goes in and out; the moon has a cycle from crescent to full and back again. We experience good times and bad times.

LAW OF CAUSE AND EFFECT

THE LAW OF Cause and Effect is also called the Law of Circulation and Exchange. We see this all the time. For every cause, there is an effect. Ralph Waldo Emerson said the Law of Cause and Effect is "the law of laws." When you learn how to use it, you can throw open the gates to receive all your desires for success.

LAW OF GENDER

THE LAW OF Gender states that it is necessary to have male and female, whether we're talking about people, plants, or animals.

EACH ONE OF these laws is unseen. Some people are reluctant to consider their effects on their personal and professional lives, but I've experienced them, and they are much more abundant and more satisfying than I could have imagined. We all believe in and know about gravity, but we don't see it. It is there and has a constant effect on every moment we are alive. It has a constant effect on everything in the universe. We don't see, taste, or smell it, but we do feel it. We use it and the other laws unconsciously everyday.

Our approach to these natural laws can make a difference in our success rate as leaders and individuals. They will continue to act, whether we tap into them consciously or not, but we can use them as assets if we so choose. I want to share the practical application as they relate to business success. I've experienced it and want to give it to others.

I want to review a few of these natural laws and invite you to consider what a difference they can make in your life. You can be wealthier than you ever imagined. You can gain anything you've ever dreamed about.

"We all work with one infinite power. We all guide ourselves by exactly the same laws. The natural laws of the universe are so precise that we don't have any difficulty building spaceships, we can send people to the moon and we can time the landing with the precision of a fraction of a second."
--Bob Proctor

WHAT YOU THINK about and focus on becomes your reality. Believe it or not, things start out as thoughts. What we can envision and dream, we can create. I'm sure you have always heard the saying that "like things attract." That is actually the basic concept of the Law of Attraction. We act like a magnet and attract everything that we need into our lives in order to accomplish our goals. If you are focusing on all the negative things that have happened in your past, you probably will continue to experience life as unsuccessful and unpleasant.

That is one of the reasons we discussed self-image first. It has a greater significance on what happens to us than many people realize. I hope you will keep reading and not set this aside because it sounds like a bunch of people sitting around thinking good thoughts. This concept is far more than that

If you've ever experienced or know someone who has experienced living from hand-to-mouth, it is not easy or what you really want. The problem is that when we are stuck in a hole, we seem to want to just keep digging deeper and deeper. We focus on the negative results we've lived with, and that actually drives what happens to us next. We might say that we want things to be different, but contrary to what we say, we continue to focus and think on negative results.

Let me put it this way. If you have one quarter of your income invested in an area in which your productivity and income decreases, do you get caught up in the feeling of failure? Do you begin running the things you did wrong over and over in your mind? Guess what? If you concentrate on the mistakes and errors you made the last quarter, you will probably repeat them.

When I worked in sales, I saw this happen over and over. People wanted to expand their sales and territories, but kept doing and thinking the same old things. Only when you change your focus will things begin to change. Surrounding yourself with negative thinking and negative people can only give you negative results. Realistically, think about it; this is not what you are in business for. You want success.

My prosperity is directly related to what I think. If I'm convinced that I can't become wealthy, then I can't. If I focus on the fact that investments are down, then I think that I can't make any money or refinance a new project for my business. Don't spend even two minutes going there. It only inhibits you from becoming all that you are capable of being.

The Law of Attraction and the Law of Vibration are related. Scientists have confirmed that everything in the universe vibrates at a particular rate. Think of tuning instruments in an orchestra. If you've ever played an instrument, you know that it can sound flat or sharp, and needs to be adjusted in order for you to play in tune with everyone else. The sound waves must match up to be in tune.

Another example is how a radio or television finds the channel you are looking for. With digital technology, we just pick a number and it comes in. However, when I was a child, radios had a dial that turned. You had to turn the dial until the frequency was just right in order to listen to a station without static or the sound cutting in and out.

The principles of the Law of Attraction originated and have been followed in Eastern cultures for centuries. Western culture has adopted its concept into New Age thinking. I realize that many Westerners have a tendency to think it's some kind of weird concept that "those strange people" believe. However, the knowledge of the Law of Attraction is becoming more and more accepted in our society. Some people who are introduced to these concepts for the first time think they are somehow inherently evil. I think that's silly to classify something that is part of nature as evil. Many of us who teach these concepts and use them in successful businesses don't consider it a contradiction of our other beliefs at all. The Laws are forces in the universe that is at work, whether you are aware of them or not.

Perhaps it may sound a little complicated to put it this way, but the metaphysical principle behind it deals with the ultimate nature of reality. It comes down to you making the choice of what to focus on.

How many times have you asked why things happen to you that you didn't want or plan? That's where we get stuck pointing our fingers, blaming other people for our circumstances. Don't you think it's interesting that some people look at situations that are bad for them and blame "bad luck"? On the other side of the coin, there are people who think that positive things are a result of "good luck." I hate to break it to those who think that way, but the reality is that it doesn't have anything to do with luck.

The truth is that your future is a product of your own thoughts. How you think about things and what you allow to be fed into your brain determines your success or failure. Whether you believe it or not, these natural laws of attraction and vibration are at work in you and everyone around you.

For those of you who are interested in science, let me explain it this way. The universe and everything in it is made up of molecules. Scientists have found that the laws governing the interaction between molecules and chemical bonds are an illustration of the natural laws we're discussing. For the rest of us, we remember learning in science class that we are made up of cells that are made up of molecules. The same motion that is a constant in those cells make up everything on our planet, you, me, the plants, animals, structures, minerals, natural resources, everything.

I've learned that the natural laws are not only physical, but they are spiritual, too. Another aspect that creates a vibration is that of feelings and emotions. When we add feelings and emotions to our thoughts, it creates a vibration that attracts like people and circumstances to us. The Law of Attraction creates a bond between you and what you need to make your thoughts into a reality. Your thoughts, your focus, others who share your thoughts, and the materials you need to be outrageously successful all vibrate to the same frequency.

Our thoughts literally send out energy and vibrations to connect with a match. That is to say, the vibration more or less seeks for something else that will resonate at the same rate and a connection is made. I'm sure you have experienced things that you thought were only coincidences. You meet someone who can help you learn what you need to in order to fulfill your goal. You are invited to attend a seminar where you find the exact answers you needed to succeed. You are reading a magazine or a book that gives you the answer you've been looking for to solve a particular problem so you can move on. This process is how it happened to me. I learned that the more aware I am of the laws and the more I consciously use them, the more successful I become.

I touched on visualization earlier in the book. Some people say that the next step after visualization is that of manifestation. Manifestation is often used in reference to the Law of Attraction. Your thoughts manifest themselves in what you create. Literally, to manifest something is to make evident or apparent to the senses. It is believed that some people have actually made something out of nothing but thoughts. Whether you believe it or not, the power of the Law of Attraction and the Law of Vibration are powerful forces that you can choose to use or ignore. Just remember that the choice you make will decide your future

I learned from Bob Proctor that the Law of Attraction affects what level of prosperity you'll acquire. The more energy you focus on prosperity, the better your personal and professional life will be. Let me warn you again that

I'm not saying you should sit around and think about a pile of money in the bank, luxury cars, and new houses. The way you think about things starts the process, but when your actions reflect your thoughts, you will attract what you need and take another key step on your way to that success. It is just a matter of shifting our perception.

I've learned that my own positive thinking creates an atmosphere that attracts the right people and tools to accomplish my goals. Another lesson I want to share with you that we will delve more deeply into during the seminar is that positive energy can't be created if all I do is just say the right things. I have to believe them. Also, the universe works on its own timetable. We tend to want to rush things. Sometimes things do happen quickly, but we can't get caught up in negative feelings and thoughts because something didn't happen exactly when we thought it should.

This book and others similar to it are written by people who are successful with these concepts and have abundant lives. They use the Law of Attraction every day. I can help you learn to incorporate it into your personal and business life and reap the benefits.

Another aspect we will work on together is to develop your belief system to include these concepts. Believe that you deserve to have prosperity and success in your life. No one is meant to be poor. We can also be rich in mind and spirit. Intentional use of the Law of Attraction brings abundance into your life.

I had experienced success in the corporate world before I learned about the natural laws and how I could use them. This new knowledge allowed me to expand and grow in every way. It is too easy for people to fall into the trap of seeing other people's achievements, wealth, or power, and wonder why it doesn't happen to them. It is a choice. Choose to see the potential, and we can grow together.

Thousands of people have learned and applied the Law of Attraction; it has worked for them and can work for you. I've studied and used my corporate knowledge as a partner with these concepts. I don't have to reinvent myself any more. You don't, either.

"All the Powers of the Universe are Already Ours,
It is We Who Have Put Our Hands Before Our Eyes and Cry that it is Dark!"
--Vivekananda (1863 – 1902)

DURING A BOB Proctor seminar I learned that because of the natural Law of Polarity, when I found myself facing a challenge or a problem, I would also receive the solution. However, I needed to be open-minded enough to see it. I enjoy helping others to discover how to use this part of the natural laws for building success and fortune. The Law of Polarity is just one more piece of the puzzle that gives us the complete picture.

If you've never heard Bob's story, it is not one of riches and privilege. He wanted more than a pension at the end of his career. He made the decision to change his life and he did. He is now wealthy and successful, and he shares these same concepts and lessons that I now share.

The images in your mind give you the energy that creates what you are receiving. If you don't like what you are getting, then this is your chance to make a change that will give you the life you've always wanted and more. You may be asking yourself that if this is basically the secret, then why should you call me and use my consulting services? That is a valid question. The answer is that applying these principles to your business and your life needs to be done in a specific way. Because I have the business experience to understand where you are professionally, I can relate to you and how you do things now. However, because I can also add the application process of these concepts to your tool kit, it is a win-win decision to contact me and use my expertise.

You may be asking yourself what does all of this have to do with creativity. It is a platform for your natural creativity. If we believe that we all have a part of God in us and that He is the master creator, then why wouldn't we also be creative? We get too wrapped up in the daily grind and forget that we can create anything we want. I know that each of us have different God-given talents that we use. Not everyone is a painter like Picasso. We don't sculpt like Michelangelo. We may not create landscaped gardens like a pro, but who is to say we couldn't if we decided to?

Creativity in business isn't limited to the website design or a brochure and catalog that you put out semi-annually. Creativity is how you view your world. It's the way you process information that is different from someone else. It is the way you solve problems. Are you open to new ideas on how to resolve your problems? Do obstacles represent opportunities to you, or are they merely something else that you think stands in your way?

How you picture your business and success in the next year or five years is a form of creativity. You see it in your mind. You dream about it at night. You work with others to see it develop. Think about Walt Disney. Disneyland and all the theme parks created by his corporation began with one thought, one creative idea. I'm not saying that you need to develop a theme park. But I'm asking you to think about what you would like to do or see.

I came across a quote from a letter written in 1818 by John Keats to James Hessey. In this letter, Keats speaks about creativity and its relationship to our willingness to step out of our comfort zone and do something to experience it in order to learn something we might not else wise have been exposed to.

". . . That which is creative must create itself – In Endymion, I leaped
headlong into the Sea, and thereby have become better acquainted
with the Soundings, the quicksands, and the rocks, than if I had
stayed upon the green shore, and piped a silly pipe,
and took tea and comfortable advice. –
I was never afraid of failure;
for I would sooner fail than not be among the greatest."
--John Keats

THE SENTIMENT OF this quote is the same today in the twenty-first century as it was in the nineteenth century. When you apply this to being open-minded enough to experiment and learn other concepts, it makes sense.

As you consider this, I'd like to share some of the questions that Bob Proctor uses before people take a seminar. They can help you in deciding to become a part of the population who enjoy wealth and success.

We start by looking back on your image and the experiences you've had in your life. You can write down notes about each question if you choose to, but what I really want you to do is consider them. Think about them.

What are your relationships like? (I know this may be a little repetitive of some of the things we've discussed other places, but it is worth giving some extra time to consider.)

Have you fallen in love recently? Are you still in love with someone?

What about your friends? What are they like?

What kind of communication do you have with family and friends?

How much money do you make each year?

Do you have your own business? What is it like? Do you work for someone else? Are you in good health?

What is your self-image of your body?

CONSIDER THE THOUGHTS that came to your mind first. Those are the ones that are programmed into your brain. They are responsible for your results. If you're not satisfied with what you've got, then it is up to you to make the changes that will give you different results.

In spite of what your desk may look like some days, the universe is an orderly place. Things that happen are not by chance or accidental. In the seminar, we will work towards developing the potential that is already within you. You will be an attractive force in the world. You will develop a successful and positive network of people around you that you may not have known existed before. It only gets better.

You may have questions of your own that you would like answered. You may find part of the answer in this book. It can be a beginning, but you will need the seminar as one of your puzzle pieces to complete the full picture. Another way to put it is the difference between a blurry picture and a digitally-enhanced, perfect picture.

I will help you through the process of finding answers to these questions and others:

What is the best path in life for me?

Is it true that there are no limitations on what I can achieve?

How exactly do I apply the natural laws to my own thought process?

What is the difference between spirituality and religion?

What does meditation have to do with my success?

How do the natural laws apply to business?

How does it work with family groups or organizations?

How do I give back to the world, and what does that have to do with it?

BECAUSE YOU ARE already a manager or a CEO of a company, this may be a process of looking at things you haven't considered in the context that I am stating. I'm sure that you've considered some of these factors before, but this is a new way to look at your world and make it a better one.

One more thing I want to discuss before we move on is that you do need to be careful what you ask for. You may have experienced a situation or known someone who asked for something and got exactly what it was they wanted. However, what they got turned into more than they originally had imagined.

I don't know about you, but I honestly believe that God has a great sense of humor. I've experienced his humor myself in business and my personal life over the past few years that I've been a consultant with this process. I've also seen others enjoy a new life. You start with the decision and follow the steps I teach and it works. Others have gone from an ordinary job to new cars, larger homes, and more successful businesses that allow them to enjoy life. Success happened for them and thousands like them, it happened for me, and best of all, it can happen to you.

I believe that most people are concerned about their financial security. This can be hard to visualize. I think you can verbalize what you want, but it's harder for some of us to actually see it in our mind's eye. Jack Canfield says that we should picture ourselves doing the things that others, who already enjoy the lifestyle we want to emulate and create for ourselves, do. Don't get too far ahead of yourself by living it and not doing the action part of your journey. Start with thoughts, and they will manifest through action and attraction to those people and things that you need in order to actually create that life.

I also think it is important that we share with others. That is one of the main reasons I am writing this book and conduct seminars, to share with others and to create a better world.

Remember that the Law of Attraction implies that anything is within the realms of possibility. However, it is dependent on your strong desires, your belief in it, and the actions you take towards your goal. It is important for you to think and plan BIG. You wouldn't want to think mediocre and get mediocre.

According to what I've learned in the coaching program, the natural laws work best if your purpose is not focused on you, but on something that will benefit others as well. Think about it. There are so many needs that should be met in the world, and you can be a part of that and enjoy living a wealthy life. As your wealth grows, it enables you to contribute to causes you've always wanted to be a part of and make a difference in many lives on a worldwide basis.

Before you spend some time on the Leadership Exercise for this chapter, I have a short list of things for you to consider:

Do you desire a more abundant life?
Would you like to earn a greater income?
Do you want to provide more for your family?
Do you sometimes worry about money?
Does the number of hours you work reflect the income you want?
Do you dream about things you want in life, but think you can't afford them?
What happens if you lose your current job?
Do you have other streams of income?

LEADERSHIP EXERCISE

In this exercise, we will briefly look at the concepts that we will focus on further in the seminar. I hope you will continue to go through these questions. They are helpful to you as a tool to help you focus on what needs I can provide for you and your organization.

What kind of competition exists in your organization? How does it affect productivity?

_____

_____

_____

_____

_____

_____

_____

What would you like to change about the competition?

_____

_____

_____

_____

_____

What goes on in your organizational culture to encourage creativity?

_____

_____

_____

_____

_____

_____

What goes on in your organizational culture to discourage creativity?

_____

_____

_____

_____

_____

Are you attracting or resisting wealth in your life? How?

_____

_____

_____

_____

_____

_____

Consider how the Law of Attraction could make a difference in your business and in your personal life. Journal your thoughts.

_____

_____

_____

_____

_____

Use the rest of this page to journal your thoughts and reactions to the questions throughout this chapter.

_____

_____

_____

_____

_____

_____

_____

_____

POINTS TO REMEMBER

- We are all creative beings.
- We are here to serve each other.
- Creativity and passion can make your business excel.
- Every accomplishment has started with a creative thought.
- The seven natural Laws of the Universe are at work in all things.
- Your approach to these natural laws is related to your success.
- Keep an open mind to possibilities.
- You haven't failed if you keep going.
- Focus on your successes.
- Learn from your mistakes and move on; don't focus on them.
- The Law of Attraction and Vibration will attract what you focus on. It will bring you what you need.
- The Law of Attraction affects your prosperity.
- It's not about just being rich; it's about the freedom to be who you were meant to be.

Chapter Eight

THE ARTICULATE
APPROACH

Chapter Eight

THE ARTICULATE APPROACH

"Our ideals resemble the stars, which illuminate the night. No one will ever be able to touch them. But the men who, like the sailors on the ocean, take them for guides, will undoubtedly reach their goal."
-- **Carl Schurz**

NOW THAT THOSE creative juices are flowing, let's talk about goal setting. I know you're probably thinking you don't have time for a simple concept. You set a goal and do what you have to in order to achieve it. However, do you have some goals that remain elusive and feel like they are just barely out of your reach? I'd like to help you change that. Stay with me and let's examine why goal setting doesn't always work as well as it should.

I'll bet you and I can think of examples of goals that you set with your organization, but weren't accomplished on the timeline you anticipated, or they were not as successful as you had planned. Some may have even failed and have been scrapped. Why do some people always reach their goals, and others experience hit-or-miss results?

Part of the answer is the way that goals are set and the way we approach the process of attaining them. In my experience, we've all been taught goal setting in one form or another. I remember the first time I saw Zig Zigler speak. Thousands of people were in attendance. I had pushed my way to the front. I didn't want to miss a thing. If you've ever seen Zig, you know that he gets down on one knee, holds out his arm, and looks right at you and says: "You've got to have a goal."

I felt like it was a one-on-one conversation between him and me. I stood there in the front row thinking, Yeah, yeah, but how do I get rich?

He was telling me, "You have to have a goal!"

I though, Yeah, okay, I understand that, but how do I get rich? I never once thought that I should go home and write down some goals. I focused on the results I wanted and didn't consider the steps I needed to take. Zig was telling me what I needed to do, but I was locked in my own thoughts and viewpoint.

Most people think that they know about goal setting. You just decide what you want to accomplish and then figure out how to get it. One of the downfalls is that those you work with can't read your mind. They can't see what you see. I've found that in many cases if you ask people to write down all that they know about goal setting, they could only fill up the back space of a postage stamp. This is because most people don't realize that there is a huge difference between goal setting and goal achievement. I used to think the two were one and the same, and then I wondered why my idea of goal setting didn't always work. Goal setting took experience, enlightening myself with new thoughts and concepts, and then applying them.

We can't see ourselves except from our own point of view. I grew up in the Midwestern United States, and my grandpa used an expression, "You can't see the forest for the trees." It is an old expression and has become cliché, but it is true. We can't see the whole picture when we are in the middle of it. I'd like you to entertain a new idea with me. We're going to touch on something that will make your goal setting not just an exercise but an achievement. I will go further in-depth during my seminar, but this will give you a start.

I believe that there are three fundamental mistakes that people and organizations make when they set goals. Companies fail miserably at this, and you have probably worked for some of them.

FIRST MISTAKE

THE FIRST MISTAKE is that companies think in reverse. They look at their results as a starting point. They allow the results that they are experiencing in their personal and professional lives to control what they think and what goal they choose. Results drive the behavior in both cases. For example, if a company is making a $1,000,000 in sales, they make a decision for the next year's goal. They announce to the employees, "Based on our current results, we know that we can hit $1.1 million in sales next year."

You may do this in your planning meetings, or you may have experienced it in other organizations. Company goals are too often based on what they know they can do. The problem with planning according to what you already know is easy to accomplish is not inspiring. It's not even challenging. When you set a goal, the purpose of it is to do two things:

It should excite you and
It should scare you.

Your goal is exciting because you want it so badly and scary because you're not sure of everything that you will need to do to accomplish it. When you set a goal, it should be a call to action. We will talk more about taking action in a later chapter. In order to achieve different results, you need to change your thought process and your actions. As we've discussed earlier, none of us like getting out of our comfort zones. Many of us don't like to do things we haven't experienced before. Meeting new people is difficult for some of us. Facing new challenges can be exciting for some and an obstacle to others. How can you overcome a situation that you've never faced before? You have to be inspired or driven by an adrenaline rush to get past it. We don't like feeling scared and will do what it takes to get out of it and back into a zone of safety.

If you are going to set goals based on what you know you can do, where is the growth? If you are going to set goals that are too low, when you reach the first obstacle that comes up, you will probably quit short of the payoff. Without inspiration and a belief in reaching your goal, what will keep you and your organization going?

"Insanity: doing the same thing over and over again and expecting different
results."
--John Dryden (from Spanish Friar,II.ii)

IT IS AMAZING how often we do the same thing we've always done and think that somehow, it will be different this time. We are then frustrated or disappointed when we keep getting the same old results and fall short of where we want to be.

SECOND MISTAKE

THE SECOND MISTAKE is not that far from the first. Our goals have evolved a little beyond basic goal setting, and we've moved to what I call a "midway position." But, the goals are still coming out of thinking in reverse. Management looks at the organization's current results first. Then, rather than setting goals on what they know they can do, they set goals based on what they think they can do.

Meetings are held and people set up all kinds of elaborate plans based on how they are going to achieve this goal. The thinking process looks something like this: if my current customers stay exactly where they are, or maybe if they spend an extra three percent, then I think I'll reach my goal. Next, we have been working on these three new accounts for the last six months, and if we can close one or two of them, then I think we can hit our goal.

The thinking process goes on to include other factors. If gas prices stay the same, then I think we can control our cash flow. If the housing bubble doesn't pop and interest rates don't go too high, then we think our plan will work. We find ourselves hoping that things go right in certain parts of the world because if they don't, that might throw more obstacles in our path. We spend weeks working out an elaborate plan that if everything goes accordingly, we will hit the goal.

The problem is that sometimes we forget the world is changing. Goals were set according to circumstances caught in a snapshot of time, but the world continues to move. The reality is that in the highly technical and instant information age we live in, conditions are in constant fluctuation. Gas prices do go up, sometimes five to ten cents in one day. The housing bubble does fluctuate. If General Motors lays off 60,000 workers one quarter, how many houses will go on the market? How does that affect the sales on the twenty houses you just built in that new community you invested in?

Regional conflicts and Middle Eastern unrest are not something we can control. It is out of the sphere of influence for most of us. We can't always predict what is going to happen, but we can look at how we handle events and how we approach goal setting. We can't always know that our customers won't renew their business next year due to unforeseen financial problems that they have experienced. Some of the prospects that you have been working with may decide that they are going to buy from their cousin's sister's brother-in-law who also sells the same widget that you sell. Maybe your competition is selling its widget for ten cents cheaper, and some of your customers buy it from them, and now the plan doesn't work, so we surrender the objective. I want to work with your organization so that you don't feel the need to surrender. Turn goal setting into goal achieving.

THE THIRD MISTAKE

THE THIRD BIG mistake people make is that they get hung up on the word "how." They will not move from their current results unless they know exactly how to get to the next level. We are so afraid to move and make the commitment. What if we make a mistake? What if we fail? What if we step out in the direction of our dream and we tell all of our friends and our family, and then fall short? We wonder, "What will they think of me?"

Believe it or not, what other people think of you is none of your business. You have control of yourself and your feelings. Others have control of theirs. What you think of you is what matters. You see, the "how" has never mattered. If you are going to set goals, but you are not moving in the direction of your goals unless you can achieve them, then stop right now and give up. It's never going to happen.

Don't get so stuck in the "how," but keep working towards your goal. If you don't know the details yet, the knowledge will come. It is part of the process to keep moving in the direction of your goals. My seminars work through this with you and your employees so that you can get the ultimate results you're after. Do you think Edison knew how he was going to illuminate the world with the light bulb at the beginning? No, but that didn't stop him from moving in the direction of his dream, did it? Do you think the Wright Brothers knew how they were going to introduce us to the age of flight?

I want to repeat this again because I think it is that important. In my own experiences, I've learned that the "how" has never mattered! It sounded strange to me at first. I couldn't understand that the particulars or individual steps didn't matter. What did matter was my keeping focused and going step-by-step and believing in myself. Seeing myself successful is what really mattered. Working with others through this process has been a great experience, and I've seen it change people and businesses for the better. The process sounds elusive at first glance, but I know how to develop it into an applicable process that will change your life.

If our goal is big enough, and it needs to be, then we are certainly going to have to "up the ante" in order to get there. Think about the solutions. Attract the solutions. Remember that the Law of Polarity provides an answer along with the problem or obstacle to your success. You may need additional education. That education can be in the form of classes or seminars. After we've taken stock of the current situation, we may be able to make improvements in our service to our clients. It may mean a big improvement in your systems. Whatever it is, don't limit yourself to small goals and become an underachiever. Create big goals and focus on them.

I am always amazed at how many companies never ask their clients or employees about their level of satisfaction. Many take the attitude if no one is complaining, then everything must be okay. How many times do we decide that if only some of them are complaining, then they must be the problem? No matter what a company is offering in terms of service or products, we are all in the service industry. Our greatest asset is our client base, and we must understand them and how we can best serve them. The most successful people I know spend an hour a day in solitude looking for ways that they can improve their service. This process is part of the solution to reaching our goals.

This poem is a good illustration of the way many of us approach our personal and professional life and when we set a goal. No wonder so many people fall short. Their expectations set them up to fall short of their goal. This poem also is an illustration of our willingness to settle for something less when we could have hit the jackpot.

"I bargained with life for a penny,
And life would pay no more,
However I begged at evening
When I counted my scanty store.
For life is a just employer
He gives you what you ask
But once you have set the wages
Why, you must bear the task

I worked for a menial's hire
Only to learn dismayed
That any wage I had asked of life
Life would have willingly paid."
-Jessie B. Rittenhouse

BECOMING A VISIONARY leader puts you into a different category than most CEOs and mangers. You are in a position not only to change your business in which you have chosen to work, but also your life! When you choose to set a BIG goal, you will be excited. That excitement, that rush will motivate your actions to do everything you can to accomplish it. As a goal achiever, you will create your own future.

As a part of the process of goal setting and achieving, you get to have life your way, not the way someone else chooses for you. Success is part of your own personal empowerment. Remember to be specific when you choose your goal. How can you ever define or achieve a vague concept or idea? Focus! Don't get led away or distracted by other people or other things to do that may pull you away from the direction you need to be traveling in to achieve your goal.

In my experience, one of the best feelings is when you've reached a goal that you had to strive for. It wasn't easy, but you did it in spite of any resistance you experienced or obstacles you had to tackle. Every time you reach your goal, your own self-confidence soars. The next time you set a goal, you know you've done it before and you can do it again. Then it becomes a track record of successfully reaching your goals. You are not simply a planner; you are an achiever!

All of the most successful business people I know are focused and dedicated. They believe in themselves and their capabilities. They believe that when they need it, the materials, resources, and people will become available to complete the project. That is one of the reasons why it is so important to set clear, well-defined goals.

In the process of accomplishing your goals, remember that there may be some smaller goals or steps within that major achievement. Celebrate them all and stay focused. That is the way your business and lifetime goals will be achieved. Everyday you should be moving closer to the end product. Working towards that end gives you a perspective that shapes your decisions and your actions along the way.

The LifeSuccess Goal Achiever Program that I have been through in my training as a consultant is an amazing process. This process has helped me to be an achiever, not just someone who sets goals that may or may not happen. While I am giving you some general tips in this chapter about goal setting and its importance in your business, there is much more to be covered in a seminar. The training I offer will give you a thorough understanding of the elements that are involved in getting the results you want. For me and many others I know, the process is literally life-changing. Did you know that only three percent of people who set goals actually write their goals down? I suspect that is one reason why they don't accomplish their goals.

The experience is much like standing in a dark room with no windows and a solid door. You can't see anything. Sometimes we find ourselves in those places. We just don't recognize things around us that can help us succeed. Then, someone opens the door and turns on the light. You may blink a few times, but everything comes into focus. There are things available to you that were in your reach, but you didn't know they were there. That's what this program is like.

I want to touch on a few basics of goal setting that you may have heard before, but may have forgotten. This is like a peek into the room where you just spent some time in the dark.

WRITE YOUR GOAL AS A POSITIVE STATEMENT

WE'VE DISCUSSED THE effect of positive energy on your results. It extends to all aspects of your life. Use statements such as, "I will achieve," or "I will earn."

BE CLEAR AND PRECISE ABOUT YOUR GOAL

USE DATES AND times to be clear what your deadline is. With a clear vision of what your goal will look like when you reach it, you will know when you've completed the job. If there are materials or personnel you know you will need to assist you, and then write them down as part of your plan. However, remember that after clearly stating your goal you don't have to know everything about the "how" part of the process at the beginning. Move towards your goal and the rest of the "how" will take care of itself.

PRIORITIZE YOUR GOALS

I CAN'T THINK of any organization that only has one thing activity or task going on at a time. I'm sure it is the same in your business. You have several goals that are works-in-progress, which can be overwhelming. That is why it is so important to prioritize them in the order of the attention they demand and how important they are to your bottom line.

WRITE YOUR GOALS DOWN ON PAPER.

WHEN WE WRITE something down on a piece of paper, it is like making a contract with ourselves. We have cemented it in place. It is real.

After you have reached your goal, take time to experience the satisfaction and joy that it brings into your life. Look at the progress you've made. Then take a look at the experience from start to finish. You may have learned something that will lead you to make adjustments on other goals. The next time can become quicker and easier if you apply the lesson learned.

I want to say one more time that your goal must be something you truly want. Don't sit back and play it safe. We've already discussed some of the payoffs for taking risks and thinking BIG. Each goal achieved moves you toward the ultimate vision and realization of your dream. Think of gaining your heart's desire.

*"We are at our very best and we are happiest when we are
fully engaged in work we enjoy on the journey toward the goal
we've established for ourselves. It gives meaning to our time off and
comfort to our sleep. It makes everything else in life
so wonderful, so worthwhile."*
--Earl Nightingale

I WANT YOU to begin the change right now. Leave the past behind and look forward to the future you are creating. Then, embrace what you really want to do and go after it with every thought and action.

LEADERSHIP EXERCISE

IN THIS EXERCISE I want you to examine and reflect on the goals you have set in the past or are currently working on. You will then move on from there. These questions will help you consider your future and how we can work together to make you a goal achiever.

What goals have you set that were not accomplished? Why? _____

_____

_____

_____

_____

_____

What process have you used in the past for setting goals? _____

_____

_____

_____

_____

_____

What would you like to change about your business, your finances, and your personal life?

_____

_____

_____

*What goals are you currently working towards achieving?*_____

_____

_____

_____

_____

*Now, dream BIG. Write down some really BIG goals for yourself.*_____

_____

_____

_____

_____

_____

POINTS TO REMEMBER

- You will never out-perform your self image, so remember you are a winner.
- There is a difference between goal setting and goal achievement.
- Set goals that reach beyond your regular performance. Aim high.
- The goals you set should either excite or scare you.
- Goals are a call to action.
- If you set goals based on current conditions, then you won't hit extraordinary results.
- Don't settle for limited expectations, creating limited results.
- Don't get too hung up on the "how" of achieving the goal.
- Other people's opinions of you don't matter.
- It's important to stay focused and believe you will reach the goal.
- Create BIG goals.
- Goal achieving builds your self-confidence and your wealth.

Chapter Nine

DECISIONS AND ACTION

Chapter Nine

DECISIONS AND ACTION

"You see, in life, lots of people know what to do, but few people actually
do what they know. Knowing is not enough. You must take action."
--Anthony Robbins

WE HAVE COVERED some familiar territory and have introduced
some principles that can make a difference. I'm sure that you read and receive
reports concerning your business everyday and use that information to make
decisions. This is not new to you. However, I would like to continue to give
you a different slant on the everyday activities of business that can change
your future only for the better, if you apply them with my assistance.

Remember how you felt when you applied for your first real job, or left
your old job for a better one, and how excited you were at the prospects for
your future. How did you feel when you first started your own business? I'm
sure that one of the first lessons you learned was that the more enthusiastic
you and those in your organization are concerning your purpose, the more
engaged the employees are in the process. Results meet your expectations.
Arnold Tynbee said, "Apathy can be overcome by enthusiasm, and enthusiasm
can only be aroused by two things: first, an ideal, which takes the imagination
by storm, and second, a definite, intelligible plan for carrying that ideal into
practice."

Everything you accomplish begins with a decision. Bob Proctor defines
it as "a single mental move you can make which, in a millisecond, will
solve enormous problems for you. It has the potential to improve almost
any personal or business situation you will ever encounter ...and it could
literally propel you down the path to incredible success." He goes on to say
that not only your income, but your whole life is dominated by the power of
your decisions. "The health of your mind and body, the well-being of your
family, your social life, and the type of relationships you develop," are a direct
reflection of the sound decisions you make.

Using the concepts and business experience I have developed over
the years, I learned that decision-making is a skill that we have to learn on
our own. It isn't part of the curriculum of our university business schools.
When we have the proper tools and information and use certain disciplines,

we become more proficient as effective decision makers. By helping you to be even better at making decisions than you already are, we can virtually eliminate confusion and conflicts that happen in your organization, thereby creating ongoing order and better results.

Even though the process of considering the information you have and figuring out how best to use it is all in your head, decision-making has a concrete and visible result. Your indecision develops internal and external conflicts. These conflicts can be defined as ambivalence. If you stay in this state of mind for very long, you tie your own hands and can stop productivity in your organization. Without clear direction, efficiency suffers throughout all levels of a business.

When we consider this information in the context of the universal law of "creation or disintegration" you can see that indecision will result in disintegration. All of us suffer from indecision or confusion at one time or another. Think about some of these and how they can affect your future:

Love 'em or leave 'em
Stay where you are or quit
Do it or don't do it
File for bankruptcy or not
Get up and go to work, or stay home and watch television
Buy something or not
Say something or not

YOU HAVE MADE decisions like these for years. Sometimes you feel confident and strong about them; other times you may feel ambivalent or even fearful. No matter how we feel as a CEO or manager, we can't avoid decisions. When we work through this together, we'll examine your good decisions and those that didn't work out as well.

Do you let the resources that are available to you dictate what the outcome will be? Think about the story we mentioned previously about President Kennedy and Werner von Braun. What was von Braun's attitude? Neither of them worried about how much it would cost to put an American on the moon. They focused on the end result. John F. Kennedy told the American public that this country would put a man on the moon in ten years. He didn't say, "We will if ..."

Once we decide to do something, conditions change. The resources that you need to fulfill your vision will come to you. You'll always find what you need, if you maintain your focus. I know that some of you or your business associates think this concept is absurd. However, I personally have experienced success in my business and want to help you apply this process in yours. I'd like for you to stop a minute and think about it. Do you want to be thinking about your limitations or your opportunities for success?

One thing we seem to let get in our way too often is circumstances. How many times do circumstances stand between you and what you want to accomplish? Don't let your dreams be shattered and your goals escape you because of conditions. Don't use circumstances as an excuse to get you off the hook from being responsible for whether or not you reach the results you truly want. I can help you learn to take charge and keep you from getting detoured by unforeseen circumstances. The great French military genius Napoleon Bonaparte said, "Circumstances, I make them." My point is that we can examine how you make decisions and view circumstances. Your viewpoint can change, if needed; it's up to you. Just make the decision and take the next step.

We talked earlier about the fear of failure. If you fail at something, it doesn't make you a failure. However, if you decide to quit, it was a conscious act of your own. Think about baseball players who have signed contracts worth millions. Do they hit the pitch for a homerun every time they step up to the plate? Do they get even a base hit every time? Everyone remembers Babe Ruth's record for hitting home runs: 714 times. People tend to forget that he struck out almost twice that number.

Thomas Edison didn't have a working light bulb the first time he attempted it, but he kept working. His decision was to succeed, and his focus was to keep at it until he did. Most people don't know that he had 10,000 failures before he succeeded in making a light bulb that actually worked. Like Edison and other inventors who had clear visions of what they wanted to accomplish, you, as a successful CEO need to maintain that same type of vision.

> *"A failure establishes only this: that our determination to succeed*
> *was not strong enough."*
> **--John Christian Bovee**

WE UNDERSTAND THAT fear is a natural emotion that protects us from danger. However, let me tie this together with the previous chapter. Fear can be a motivator. The problem with stepping outside of our comfort zone is that people imagine danger that doesn't actually exist. They confuse fear with risk. It can be paralyzing.

If you allow yourself to get caught up in it, fear can limit you and keep you from making the right decision at the right time. Sometimes it is a matter of old fears from our past projected onto a new situation that we haven't experienced before. Negative energy gets stronger and stronger with this type of mindset.

I want to stop and consider risk-taking because it is a part of your decision-making process. It's an integral part of daily business. We need to be positive, but we also need to intelligently manage our risk factors by being informed. When you think of the word "risk," it has negative connotations. We think it somehow implies danger, tension, and the possibility of loss. However, risk does have a positive side. Your long-term payoffs should be worth any short-term prices. The end result is abundance.

As you know, there are two types of risk, intelligent risks and ill-advised risks. Nothing about them indicates that it is a good idea. In some cases, people lose more than they can afford. I heard someone say one time that you should never risk more than you are willing to lose. I know that is a negative statement, but it is something to consider. Bob Proctor advises people to be willing to make sacrifices to get what you want, but not to put themselves in a position that you cannot take care of your needs and your family's needs. Take care of the basics. Then, let's go out and take some risks that will create a wonderful future.

The most intelligent risks are those where the potential downside is limited, but the potential upside is virtually unlimited. Those are the risks you should jump to take. Don't miss the big chances in life to excel by giving in to fear. Think about some examples. When is the last time you asked someone out on a date? We've all experienced the downside of that experience. You might embarrass yourself by stumbling over your tongue. You could be rejected. However, if you don't ask, you may miss out on the relationship of a lifetime. This person could be your soul mate and best friend.

What about the last time you applied for a higher paying position at work? The downside could be that you don't get an interview, or you do get one, but blow it and don't get the opportunity. You could be rejected despite your qualifications. The upside is that you may land the ideal job you've been working for. If you don't apply, you won't get the raise and the promotion. You will be able to do things you haven't before because you've brought more abundance into your life through this promotion.

Decide to open yourself up for new concepts that can change your life and that of your business. The downside is you'll spend some time out of your schedule learning and reading about a more abundant life. You may meet resistance from friends and associates along the way. The upside is you'll spend time in a seminar, but this isn't just any seminar that can't hold your attention. What I'm offering is life-changing. For me, it opened up possibilities that I would have never imagined. It took my success and made it exponentially larger, both in my finances and my quality of life.

In my experience, becoming a consultant with Bob Proctor's philosophy was the best decision I've ever made, except for saying "yes" when my husband proposed. How many times have you been invited to some seminar where people just stood up in front of the room like cheerleaders as a state championship pep rally? Everyone leaves motivated and excited, but there is no substance to take with you and apply. The great thing about my concepts and methods are that they get results. I admit that some people will walk away without taking the risk, and that is their choice. Others may attend but not "get it." They don't want to do something different and will continue to get the same old results. The rest of you will experience the long-term payoff with the best outcome by taking the gems with you. This successful group can create permanent change for themselves and the world around them. It is a matter of personal and professional growth, all wrapped up in the same package.

As a LifeSuccess Consultant, I receive a daily insight from Bob Proctor. I received this one while writing this book and feel it is a perfect illustration of what I'm trying to share with you:

"Several years ago, I read an excellent book on the subject of risk-taking. It was entitled The Young Millionaires, and it contained the true-life stories of eighteen individuals, each of whom had earned in excess of one million dollars. In fact, some of these people had actually earned many millions of dollars, over and above the one million dollar mark, during the course of their highly successful careers. Throughout the book, the author made many interesting observations about the 'law of financial success,' but the most important one was the one which he kept coming back to: namely, although these individuals came from a variety of different backgrounds, and although each had earned their money in a different way, they all shared one thing in common."

What was that one thing, you may ask. Simply put it was this: even though everything they owned was riding on the outcome of virtually every major business decision they made, none of them considered themselves to be taking "risks." The reason they didn't," Bob went on to explain, was because they were living their lives "as though it were impossible to fail!"

Another key in the process is to learn to make decisions in advance. We go into this in-depth during the seminar, but I want you to think about it. It can be as simple as making reservations for a flight and hotel for a seminar I am planning to hold in two months. It centers on the way you think and the way you apply those thoughts to your business commitments and goals. We can work together to take this concept and temper it with self-discipline.

Dr. Abraham Maslow, whose work I cited earlier in the book, spent years studying human behavior and self-actualization. His work showed that people who are decision makers like you have certain factors in common. They felt that their work was important and a worthwhile cause. Most found their jobs to be pleasurable. They enjoyed their work as much as the activities they did for fun. Their value system was one of their own choosing. Conditions in their lives, whether personal or professional, were something that they chose rather than having been imposed on them by family or members of society.

"If we all did the things we are capable of doing, we would literally astound ourselves."
--Thomas Edison

WE'VE DISCUSSED THE decision half of success, but words without actions won't get you and your organization very far, as you well know. The decisions to do nothing today mean you're automatically denying yourself possible long-term benefits. If you do nothing, that isn't a neutral stance; it is a decision not to act, not to experience what life could really be. Besides, it's negative to do nothing to further your growth.

It's amazing how much long-term difference I've experienced with just a small change that I started a few years ago. If I make one small change everyday, imagine the ultimate difference. I have set things in motion for the years to come. It took me a little self-discipline and courage to get started. Persistence is part of it, but positive enthusiasm for this path I'm on wakes me up every morning.

The best thing I can tell you at this point is to start today. Words without actions are nothing. You and I have the ability to change ourselves. By changing ourselves, we change the world around us for the better. We possess power within us to create our own future. Get past all that negative stuff. Leave it behind. Don't let your past haunt you. Keep your eyes looking forward. Keep the lessons. Dump the garbage.

When you're dumping the garbage, you're getting rid of regret, indecision, and the fears we've mentioned. First, let's consider regret. It is negative, and it gets to all of us sometimes. An acquaintance of mine defines it as the "would-a, could-a, should-a" syndrome. Hindsight is always 20/20. Our future has some aspects that are not as clear as we would like for them to be. That is part of what I'm trying to help you change. We've partially explored the concepts behind creating your own future and are close to applying them.

Regrets are like boxes on the top shelf of a storage closet. Each box represents unfinished business, parts of projects that got stalled in the middle, dreams that have been forgotten, relics of relationships that didn't work out, and plans that never made it to completion. Sound familiar?

Somewhere in the back of your mind are the feelings and personal dialogue that go along with those boxes. There may be a few you would like to keep buried, but they come back to haunt your thoughts. They even cause you to hesitate in moving forward with new projects. As we've said before, you have the power to close the door on these thoughts and get on with your future.

Let's acknowledge some of those old tapes that play in your head that come with the storage boxes:

I should've tried harder.
I could've tried harder, but ...
I should've known better.
If I had looked, I would've seen it.
I would've done it, but _____ got in my way.
If someone had told me, then I_____.
I should've finished _____.
I should've been smarter.

THESE TYPES OF thought patterns can be destructive. They blind you to possibilities because you're so busy looking backwards instead of forward. From this point on, I've found it is better choosing the life you want rather than being stuck in a circular driveway. Focus on what you want. If you don't learn to let go of the past, sooner or later it will overwhelm your present and define your future.

Getting locked into patterns of indecision can also be devastating to you and your business. Unfortunately, many of us are caught in this pattern of reality. It keeps us from progressing and from experiencing the wealthy life we could experience. These patterns keep us inside a self-made cage. Only we hold the keys to let ourselves out. In most cases, the door is open; we only choose not to go through it.

Like regrets, indecision has its own dialogue. We play this dialogue over and over in our thoughts until we believe it. We allow these thoughts to catch us like a spider web. We forget that we have the power to choose something else for ourselves. One of the biggest problems we face while stuck in this web is that by not making any decisions, we give up control to outside forces that may take us someplace we don't want to go. Be assertive. Take charge of yourself. Don't get so caught up in the "right decision" or the "wrong decision."

This negative dialogue is somewhat like the regret dialogue, except that regret relates to the past, while indecision relates to the present and impacts the future.

(You may remember this one from early in your career:) I'm so overloaded at work that I don't have time to get all my projects completed. I don't know what to do about it. Do I ask for help? Will I get fired if I don't do all of it correctly?

I really dislike my job. I don't like the people, the hours, or the schedule. I want another job with better hours so I can see my family. Can I afford to quit before I have a new job? What will I do for money? What should I do?

My business is not successful like I had hoped. Do I try to fix it? Do I just give up and file bankruptcy? Can I turn it into a money maker? I don't know what to do to change things. Should I do anything?

The best way to deal with indecision is focus. Focus on the solutions instead of the problems. As in the Law of Polarity, you have the answer available to you. You just need to be open to it. Make the conscious effort to push away anything that threatens to stand in the way of success. You are master of yourself and your future.

LEADERSHIP EXERCISE

THIS IS THE last leadership exercise. The next chapter is the call to action. Complete these questions and review the other exercises. They will help you to come to the decision of whether or not to embrace these concepts and let me guide you to a more successful life.

How do you usually make decisions? What process do you use?

_____

_____

_____

_____

_____

What scares you about decision-making? _____

_____

_____

_____

_____

_____

Are you a risk-taker? What kinds of risks are you willing to take?

_____

_____

_____

_____

_____

_____

_____

What obstacles hinder your decision-making?

_____

_____

_____

_____

_____

Do you make excuses? If yes, what? If no, what keeps you focused?

_____

_____

_____

_____

_____

_____

Brainstorm options that are available to you to solve problems that you face. Write down as many as you can.

_____

_____

_____

_____

_____

_____

POINTS TO REMEMBER

- Everything you do starts with a decision.
- Creation or disintegration is a natural law.
- Indecision will result in disintegration.
- Resources or circumstances should not limit your outcome. Remember Warner von Braun's response to President John F. Kennedy.
- Once you make a decision, conditions change.
- Take action; don't make excuses.
- Use fear as a motivator rather than letting it paralyze your progress.
- Be willing to take intelligent risks.
- Only accept limitations in the downside aspects of a decision.
- Potential is unlimited.
- Regrets over your past don't have to become obstacles to your future.
- You can overcome indecision with focus.
- Take charge. Make the decisions you need to make.

Chapter Ten

THE BOTTOM LINE

Chapter Ten

THE BOTTOM LINE

"By the choices and acts of our lives, we create the person that we are and the faces that we wear. By the choices and acts of our lives, we give to the world wherein our lives are lived, hoping that our neighbors will find our contributions to be of worth, and hoping that the world will be a little more gracious for our time in it."
--**Kenneth Patton (adapted)**

THE BOTTOM LINE is your real target. How does this information help you? First, I have the corporate and marketing experience, as well as coaching and seminar experience to know what I am talking about. Second, I believe that I can help you learn and apply a more efficient way of setting goals and achieving them. Third, I have learned through business and life experiences that we receive the experience first and then learn the lesson. If we don't learn the lesson the first time, then we go through the same circumstances over and over again until we do learn it and can move forward. I don't know about you, but I would rather move closer to my goals than be stuck in what can become a quagmire of circumstances that form an even larger obstacle to my success.

LifeSuccess Consultants worldwide are personally trained and supported by Bob Proctor and Paul Martinelli. We work together and cooperate with each other to address clients' requirements. That means when you employ my services, you also employ the LifeSuccess Consultants network. As a start towards shifting the thought process, all of us offer a free ten-week book study based on Napoleon Hill's Think & Grow Rich. This is the book that changed Bob Proctor's life, and it is the cornerstone of the LifeSuccess consultants' organization.

As a CEO or manager, I'm sure you are most concerned about what the financial bottom line is every day. You seek out answers for problems that may start small and build into a crisis before they can be handled properly. How often is your organization proactive rather than reactive?

My personal philosophy is based on doing the best I can for myself, my family, my business, my clients, and my world. The overview of principles contained in this book are meant to be a starting point for you to see things from a new slant that can only make you more successful. My seminars include empowering individuals and the organization as a whole. I want to help you fill in the gaps and work with you to see how when problems arise, the answer comes with them. You just have to know how to change your perception.

I am a student of the philosophy Dr. Carl Jung and have learned many things that apply to business and life in general.

> *"Every advance, every achievement of mankind, has been*
> *connected with an advance in self awareness."*
> **--C. G. Jung, Psychological Reflections**

WITH OVER TWENTY-FIVE years of sales and entrepreneurial experience, I represent a viewpoint that covers several perspectives. I've experienced corporate America, and have lived and worked in Zimbabwe, Ireland, England, and Austria. While in London, my coaching and consulting practice was mainly centered on developing business plans for small to medium sized companies. It was a mix of new start-ups to existing companies that needed help in order to go to the next level. This experience has broadened my knowledge in being able to analyze businesses in order to develop strategies that would quickly and effectively change the direction of those businesses. I was active with the Business Network International, a worldwide business referral organization, and a Registered Business Consultant with Business Link, now known as the London Development Agency, helping many of their members grow their businesses. I've received many awards over the years for sales and for working as a team player, but my greatest pleasure comes in assisting other companies to win.

AMONG MY PROFESSIONAL
QUALIFICATIONS ARE THE FOLLOWING:

Master Coach, LifeSuccess Coaching & Consulting Program
LifeSuccess Consultant
Licensee, LifeSuccess Massachusetts
Accredited Insights Associate (AIA)
Advisory Board Member, CoachLab International
Certified Coach/Lifetime Member of CoachLab International
(the Society of Professional Coaches)
Registered Consultant with Business Link UK

ONE OF THE things that distinguishes me from others is my international experience in the corporate world and expertise in executive coaching. My seminars reach the corporate itch that is difficult to scratch.

In 2005, I was in a certification program in London to become a LifeSuccess consultant. LifeSuccess Productions is an American company, run by two partners who are business leaders and are at the forefront of changing how business is being done.

Although I have a coaching certification from another organization, I have been studying and following Bob Proctor for a couple of years. I was particularly attracted to Bob's programs because they are the only ones I know of that teach people how to actually achieve sustained change. It is this difference that makes LifeSuccess stand out from other motivational programs. I believe that, without question, Bob is one of the best coaches in the world today, and the fees that he commands would be proof of many other people's opinions as well. The list of top companies that have hired Bob to teach them how to get better results in the long run. I found that the more I studied his work and his methods, the better my results were, so much so that I wanted to be certified to deliver his programs. That is what I am offering to you and your organization.

Like you, I absolutely love success, in athletics, for my children, and in all aspects of life. I just love watching it happen. I have been in pursuit of success all my life, and combining my past experiences with Bob Proctor's concepts has made a huge difference. I've reached goals and success far beyond where I would have on my own.

As a LifeSuccess consultant, I believe that people are motivated. It is just that they don't know what is holding them back. Our programs are effective and get to the heart of what has been preventing us from doing what we know. The process actually unlocks the power of other training programs that your company has implemented but never realized expected results from.

Furthermore, I have always been involved in personal development. I have attended seminars and purchased tapes and books on selling, business, marketing, the list goes on. I've studied everything from Anthony Robbins to Zig Ziglar, or as I say, everything from A to Z. I was fortunate enough two years ago to be invited to join a coaching program run by Bob Proctor called Lead the Field. Lead the Field was originally developed by Earl Nightingale (you may know about it), and Bob has been studying this program for more than forty years. I don't think anyone knows the program better than him. I wanted to be a part of that and be able to pass it on to others.

After the first phone call, I instantly knew that this was the guy that had the answers I was looking for. Right then, I decided I was going to study these concepts, learn them, and apply them to my own life. Since then, I've studied the material on a daily basis and listened to Bob in the weekly coaching calls. My business has grown, and I've been coaching and conducting seminars helping other peoples' businesses grow by using the same principles.

At the same time, though, if I look back over the years I spent in selling and in business, I can see that the world has truly changed. Business is not conducted in the same way at all. Sometimes in order to survive, it is necessary to reinvent yourself to adjust to the shifting times. If someone is doing business the same way that they did even five years ago, I can assure you that they are not as successful as they could be. If we look behind us all the time so that we can make advances in business, we are going to find ourselves someplace we didn't intend to go.

The pattern of looking backwards is much like trying to drive your car forwards but staring into the rear view mirror. Your mistakes lie behind you. Let them go. Look forward with a new approach to design your future. In order to keep up, we have to be willing to entertain new ideas, new concepts, and new ways of doing things.

I believe the key is continuing to educate ourselves and continual self-development. We refer to people being educated, but in fact, we never stop learning. It is a lifelong process, a journey that has no end. We are either learning, or we are standing still. The world you and I were born into is not the same world that we live in today, and the technological changes have come so much faster than our parents' generation ever had to deal with. I also believe that the marriage between my business and marketing background and the Bob Proctor way is the best combination for success available, and I want to share that with you. In Chapter Six, Bridging the Gap, we discussed how this process will help you do just that. Realize that the biggest gap is the one between what you know and what you do. We have a program that can help people move from knowing to doing. That is the way to make the changes you want.

Most of my career has been spent in the high-tech industry. I started out selling copiers and remember when only two people left the company to sell Motorola mobile telephones. At that time, no one actually knew what a mobile phone was. These ladies were tracking down guys on construction sites in the middle of nowhere. That's where the market was. People out in the field or away from home offices needed to be able to make and take phone calls in remote areas. Those first mobile phones were nothing like our tiny cell phones now.

The original mobile phones were larger than our home phones. Sales representatives had to carry them in heavy carrying cases so they could demonstrate them in the field. It was like dragging luggage around. Each phone was transported in a case that was about the size of a carry-on case when you fly. The case held everything that was needed in order for the phones to work in remote areas.

Today we have phones that are the size of a business card. For example, I could take your picture, access the Internet, log onto our email, and send information to my sister in South Carolina. If she doesn't get it in about three seconds, then I'll use the same cell phone to call a service center in India or Pakistan and they will fix the problem in the snap of a finger. If it doesn't happen that fast, I get upset and consider taking our business somewhere else.

The concepts in this book will work for everyone and every organization. I will show you strategies that will help people bridge the gap between where they are now and where they want to be in their quest. Two important qualities we've discussed are worth touching on one more time.

Persistence: It is not only crucial to reaching goals, but also in creating new behaviors and new approaches. Don't let yourself fall back into the old ways that deprive you of satisfaction and success.

Resilience: The ability to get back up again when you've been knocked down is also important to your success. Get up and completely believe that what you want is on its way to you.

REMEMBER: ABSENCE OF EVIDENCE IS NOT EVIDENCE OF ABSENCE!

SET HUGE GOALS, and I will assist you in reaching them. You will need to make bold moves, take big risks, and try new things. The trick is to control your fear instead of letting it control you. Don't be one of those people who regret having not made the choice to change. Don't allow fears to stop you in your tracks before you even get started on the path to your dreams. Sometimes people stop and rationalize, which translates to "rashing lies." Avoid making excuses that will keep you from realizing your goals.

Instead, you can be the kind of leader who creates an environment that fosters the creative powers that are within all of us and allows us to get what we want. Abraham Maslow said, "If you plan on being anything less than you are capable of being, you will probably be unhappy all the days of your life." Indeed, attitude and morale filter down from the top.

This is truly a changing world and nobody can afford to stop learning. There is a great book called True Believers written by Eric Hoffer, and in it he said this: "That in the times of change, the learners will inherit the earth, while the learned will find themselves beautifully equipped to handle the world that no longer exists." And that's true! We have to continue to learn. We have to be open-minded to new ideas and that is really all that I ask of you.

The future is in your hands. I invite you to pick up the phone and contact me. I look forward to hearing from you soon.

CONTACT ME:

www.susanbagyura.lifesuccessconsultants.com

susanbagyura@lifesuccessconsultants.com

"Pass Your Leadership On"
with Robert Sams & My Son Jackie

"Our greatest excitements and our addictions are to inspire great leaders like you to pass your success, joy, and leadership to the young leaders like you!"

"My lifetime exclusive commitment as your mentor is to empower, communicate, and develop relationship with you based on your leadership needs, desires, and wants!" *Robert*

You are going to live & learn how:*

> To stop chasing people into what you have...
>> Now attract great leaders like yourself using **"My Story Marketing"**
> To stop worrying about becoming someone you are not...
>> Now be you by choosing **"Human Being instead of Human Becoming"**
> To stop being on time and off purpose...
>> Now be **"Off Schedule and Be On Purpose"**
> To stop chasing money and status at the expense of your lifestyle...
>> Now create **"New Rich Lifestyle by Design"**
> To stop being just busy with ineffective actions...
>> Now act in a certain way to enjoy your **"Predictable Success"**
> To stop online failure and expensive campaign...
>> Now create **"Massive Online Success"** with 6 proven steps
> To stop imposing your will on people...
>> Now **"Inspire Leaders"** by being a passionate leader yourself
> To stop taking risk on luck...
>> Now live your life by **"the Law of Inevitability"**
> To stop worrying about not enough money in the past...
>> Now keep your focus on **"Adding Massive Use Value"** in the present
> To stop competing to get in the next biggest opportunity based on greed.
>> Now create **"Wealth out of Nothing"** with gratitude and grace
> To stop the ups and downs by being alone without support...
>> Now mastermind with top leaders to **"Keep and Grow Your Wealth"**

But wait... there is more! (These are only the tip of the iceberg)*
Hurry; here is my one time exclusive offer for every **"visionary leader"** book you preorder to pass it on, I will give you one hour mentorship ($597.00 value) completely on me! (101 books maximum for the first 101 leaders only) forgive me in advance if you did not make the first 101 leaders!
To Reserve Your Mentorship & Free Bonus Call @ 1-206-222-2753
Visit: **www.channelofabundance.com**

THE VISIONARY LEADER: HOW TO INSPIRE SUCCESS FROM THE TOP DOWN

AVAILABLE IN 2008

Susan Bagyura blends professional advice with straightforward explanations and the result is the understanding of the effective way to lead, which also fosters creativity and intellectual growth. She will guide you through the process of:

What you can do to access and then bridge the gap between what you know to do and what you are actually doing.

Learn how to tap into your creativity and those around you and leave the competition behind.

Learn how to avoid the 3 major mistakes people make when setting goals and then watch the quantum leaps in performance.

And so much more!

IN LIFE WE are sometimes scared or unsure of how to move forward, we have been taught to often to put away our own dreams to focus on "the real world". My desire is to show you how to bring your dreams to life. I work with individuals and companies coaching them on how to be, do and have what they desire, or give seminars on the products and information you will fall in love with in this book. My personal desire is to show people how to live up to there unlimited possibilities and unlock the uniqueness we all have within us. I would love the opportunity to show you how you can have a fuller richer life or company. What I am offering benefits all, think about your staff if they were happier wouldn't they produce better for your company? If you were happier wouldn't everything in your life move at a smoother pace? Let me help make it happen for you!

GET THE RESULTS YOU WANT
EMAIL TODAY!

EMAIL
susanbagyura@LifeSuccessconsultants.com

THE ULTIMATE TOOL for any commissioned salesperson or those working in a service industry. With simple step-by-step instructions, Bob Proctor takes you to a 6 or 7-figure income without working any harder. As you get involved in this program, you will find yourself finally and forever stepping across the line that separates so many struggling salespeople from those who win big – month after month and year after year. You will learn the six basic concepts you MUST understand before you will ever learn large commissions, and the one fundamental step you must develop to earn $100,000+ while still enjoying your work.

$195.00 U.S. available online at
www.susanbagyura.LifeSuccessconsultants.com

OFFERS A THOROUGH understanding of how each element of your being works to bring about the results you are currently getting in your life and to move towards what you truly desire. You will gain the power to transform your life into anything you choose by setting goals that you really want, prioritizing them and then learning the focus and action skills to achieve one after another. You will learn how to repeat the process. This program will take you step-by-step directly towards any goal you truly desire.

$195.00 U.S. available online at
www.susanbagyura.LifeSuccessconsultants.com

YOUR SELF-IMAGE is like the thermostat in your home – try to obtain success without adjusting your self-image and it will bring you right back to where it has been 'set' by others in the past. This program is key to building confidence in adults and teens alike. This is a strong action-oriented program with powerful emphasis on accountability. With THIS change, nothing will change in your life! The Winner's Image teaches you that you can shift and choose more beneficial power in you life by shifting how you perceive yourself first.

$195.00 U.S. available online at
www.susanbagyura.LifeSuccessconsultants.com

ARRANGING FOR YOUR own success is like putting a puzzle together. You use the picture on the box to know where the pieces to go. Without a clear, defined picture of your success you have no idea where the pieces of your life should go. This program develops that picture with your help. With this Success Puzzle Program, you'll be finding, recognizing and putting in place every piece you need to create a much more successful life. You will learn how to eliminate all obstacles blocking the paths to your dreams and goals, then study and implement the most foundational pieces that begin to build your own success picture.

$195.00 U.S. available online at
www.susanbagyura.LifeSuccessconsultants.com

HERE'S WHAT YOU WILL GET...

1. Never-Before-Recorded Audio Instruction
    With this program, you will be one of the privileged few to get access to never-before-recorded audio instruction and summaries of lessons and observations from the Teachers Bob Proctor and Jack Canfield.
    This is 10 audio CDs jam packed with their tutelage.

2. Bob Proctor and Jack Canfield, always by your side.
    We will also give you a compact digital MP3 player pre-loaded with 15-hours of content which means you will be totally immersed in the program IMMEDIATELY and CONSTANTLY to ensure you effect the Law of Attraction to bring you wealth EVERYDAY!
    Immerse yourself anytime and anywhere! Listen anytime while in a bus, on a train, waiting in line, during lunch breaks, by the pool...

3. Tools To Help You Take Action and Keep It Going
    15 Dynamic Lessons that capture specific teachings to help you further understand and implement the Law of Attraction as well as other Universal Laws. Clearly taught by Bob Proctor and Summarized by Jack Canfield.

Compact Personal Vision Boards for mapping out and envisioning the life you seek to attract.

Multiple Sources of Income (MSI) Whiteboards that motivate and inspire you to create New Channels of Wealth.

A Science of Getting Rich Goal Card - one of the primary foundational pieces in the absolute realization of your dreams.

4. New Opportunities, A Support System, Continuous Learning
   $500 Gift Certificate to attend a live seminar worldwide to continue learning in a live seminar environment!

   Instant and Global Connections for all your networking and connection needs. It's online, active communities, masterminds, blogs and discussion boards that welcome your participation and insights as you grow through this tremendous process.

   The Original Science of Getting Rich Book beautifully redesigned for this Briefcase, which means that ANYONE can master and internalize the wisdom of the ORIGINAL text without exception!

5. A Complete Training System in One Powerful Briefcase
   A Rich, Supple Leather-Bound Briefcase specially designed to contain The Home Seminar Kit so that you can take it with you EVERYWHERE with no hassle. ALL THIS Delivered to your doorstep.

ORDER YOUR BRIEFCASE TODAY AT:

www.susanbagyura.LifeSuccessconsultants.com

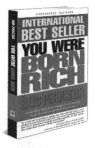

You Were Born Rich

Bob Proctor
ISBN # 978-0-9656264-1-5

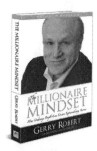

The Millionaire Mindset
*How Ordinary People Can
Create Extraordinary Income*

Gerry Robert
ISBN # 978-1-59930-030-6

Rekindle The Magic In
Your Relationship
Making Love Work

Anita Jackson
ISBN # 978-1-59930-041-2

Finding The Bloom of
The Cactus Generation
*Improving the quality of
life for Seniors*

Maggie Walters
ISBN # 978-1-59930-011-5

The Beverly Hills Shape
The Truth About Plastic Surgery

Dr. Stuart Linder
ISBN # 978-1-59930-049-8

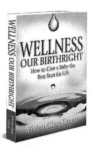

Wellness Our Birthright
*How to give a baby the best
start in life.*

Vivien Clere Green
ISBN # 978-1-59930-020-7

Lighten Your Load

Peter Field
ISBN # 978-1-59930-000-9

Change & How To
Survive In The New
Economy
*7 steps to finding freedom
& escaping the rat race*

Barrie Day
ISBN # 978-1-59930-015-3